PORTL...   :P

a walking guide to scenic and historic points of interest

The Touchstone Press
P.O. Box 81
Beaverton, Oregon 97075

Copyright © 1988
Joe Bianco
I.S.B.N. 0-911518-79-7

*This book is dedicated to Martha and Joey
whose love and respect of our environment
is a testimony to the teachings
and love of their mother,
and to my father, in his 90th year,
still a daily walker.*

INTRODUCTION

I am a walker. At heart, I am a tourist. When I visit a city I want to know about its history. I want to see everything.

I also love to see change. I get excited when I see a new building going up. I am equally thrilled when a neglected building with an historic past becomes a love affair for a caring architect who wants to bring new life to a scarred mass of stone and steel.

I want to know the special features of certain districts of a city. I want to get lost in the romance of its past but I don't want to go around in circles.

I came to Portland when Portlanders called the Pacific Power and Light Building at Southwest 6th and Taylor, with all its 15 floors, a "skyscraper." Over the years, I discovered a little bit of Paris here. Even a touch of old New York, if you close your eyes and imagine Northwest Twenty Third Avenue as another Lexington Avenue. I sometimes get a bit misty-eyed when I stroll the northwest Portland neighborhood and wander into the many little shops which remind me of South Orange, New Jersey, the village where I used to go when I was a small boy.

Although the Willamette River is a far cry from the Tiber, it can begin to suggest a slice of the Seine, if you know where to look and let your imagination take you there.

This is a book for walkers, for Portlanders as well as for tourists. I wrote it so you can learn as much as possible about my city, Portland, Oregon. It is a city that I have come to love, a romance that developed as I courted her in my walks.

Use it and you will find it is more than just a beautifully produced and entertainingly written guide book. Follow me and I will take you around Portland step by step, will show you a city that is not only nice to look at but can be a little naughty, and I will not leave you standing on a street corner somewhere, wondering where to go next.

We will go up into our southwest hills where you will see some of the grand homes, beautiful parks and a mansion or two. From there, we can meander down through the central city, or walk at a fast clip, whatever suits you.

We will walk by tall buildings which can cool you during the noonday sun or offer you a temporary shelter during one of our displays of liquid sunshine.

We will go to the Rose Gardens, where flowers of every pattern form an endless quilt of color for you to enjoy.

There will be a bit of early history throughout our travels to make the passage more interesting for those who want to linger awhile and compare what is with what was. For those who wish to quicken their gait and pulse, this book makes it possible to consume those awful calories which are so easy to attract but so formidable to conquer. If you want to stay healthy, all you need to do is burn up to 2,000 calories a week above your normal activity, providing you maintain a healthy diet.

The walks are designated according to three classes:
A. Easy, level terrain, distance under 2 miles.
B. Slightly elevated terrain, distance 2-4 miles.
C. Some steep terrain, distance 4 miles or more.

Nathan Pritikin, the world-renowned food and diet expert, told me when I interviewed him in Santa Monica some years ago, that a person should walk at least one hour each day. He recommended that to his patients who had weight problems. He suggested a half hour walk in the morning and the same for the evening. This regimen he prescribed for those in post-operative heart care. In addition, his patients had to follow a strict nutritional diet. Walking, to Pritikin, was the elixir of life.

There are many benefits to walking.

Experts like Pritikin and Dr. John Pleas, author of *Walking* and others, have told us that walking increases confidence and reduces tension, that walking also helps solve problems and is ideal for handling anger. Walking allows time to stimulate the imagination. It keeps the walker alert mentally as well as unclogging the mind. It reduces boredom. Last, certainly not least, walking makes a person self-reliant.

Throughout history some of our great leaders have been proponents of walking. President

Harry S. Truman daily took his "constitutional," pursued by a panting press, eager to gobble up a juicy Trumanism.

Even our literary greats loved to walk. George Bernard Shaw was an early devotee of walking. It seemed to have rewarded him with a lean frame, much to the envy of his frequent adversary, G. K. Chesterton, who often chided Shaw on his appearance.

A story has it that on one of their encounters, Chesterton commented on Shaw's thinness, "George, it seems as if you have been struck by famine."

Shaw countered, mockingly, to a rotund Chesterton, "It seems that you have caused it."

Although walking has not turned me into a rail, it has done wonders for my legs, short as they may be. I have concentrated almost totally on walking as a physical exercise to maintain the proper proportions for my 5 foot, 6 inch frame.

I am of Italian heritage and have the appetite that goes with it. In addition, I happen to be an amateur cook with a weakness for pasta. Despite my graying hair and the fact I belong to the generation which grew up with depression-era WPA and NRA, I have stayed continually active. While walking is my principal exercise, I ski in winter, swim, bicycle and hike and enjoy an evening in front of the tube. Walking, however, has been my saving grace.

Even my father continues to be an avid walker. He abandoned his Pierce-Arrow auto when I was a child. From that day until now he loves to walk. At 89, he said the most interesting thing about walking is that, while you may have been over the same route many times, you never see the same thing twice.

PORTLAND: PRACTICAL INFORMATION

Everyone has heard Portlanders have webbed feet. Whenever Portland is mentioned in a conversation with visitors the question that always comes up is: "Doesn't it always rain in Portland?"

Portlanders may sound defensive when they reply: "What you see is not rain but liquid sunshine."

It may seem to our visitors that it rains often, but factually speaking, New York City has more rain than we do. The annual rainfall in Portland is 37.8 inches while in the "Big Apple" it is more than 44 inches per year. Our rainfall doesn't come in buckets but is spread evenly through most of the year, accounting for our prolonged gray and wet look during the early spring and fall and winter months.

According to the weather bureau the mean January rainfall is 5.7 inches; in February, 4.17 inches; March, 3.6 inches; April, 2.25 inches; May, 2.07 inches; June, 1.5 inches; July, .55 inches; August, 1.02 inches; September, 1.71 inches; October, 3.29 inches; November, 5.5 inches; and December, 6.3 inches. That's not too awfully wet.

Portland has a moderate climate with the annual mean temperature around 52 degrees. Our temperatures range from not very cold to not very hot.

In January, the temperature averages about 38 degrees; February, it is 43 degrees; March, 46 degrees; April, 50 degrees; May, 57 degrees; June, 60 degrees; July, 66 degrees; August, sometimes the hottest month but not always, the average is 66 degrees; September, 62 degrees; October, 54 degrees; November, 54 degrees; and in December, 41 degrees. There are a few weeks when the temperatures will stay in the 90s and higher.

Now that we have the temperatures and the rainfall taken care of, let's look at some of the top sightseeing attractions which may interest you if you are a visitor or resident who wants to know more about your city.

I feel you would enjoy those attractions which truly reflect the personality of Portlanders.

We're proud of Washington Park as we are of all our parks, but more particularly we have a soft spot for this southwest Portland park which sits on a hillside overlooking most of the city. It has the renowned International Rose test gardens, the Japanese Gardens and the Washington Park Zoo, which is the home of our famous elephant herd. Included in this complex is the World Forestry Center, dedicated to our leading industry—lumber.

In the northeast section of the city at Northeast Eighty-Second Avenue and Sandy Boulevard is the nationally famous Grotto, the Sanctuary of Our Sorrowful Mother Shrine.

In the heart of the central city is the Oregon Art Institute which houses the Art Museum, the art school and the Northwest Film Study Center. Across the street from the Art Institute is the Oregon Historical Society, with its treasures of Oregon artifacts.

The walks in this book are arranged in such a manner that all of these sightseeing attractions are included in one or more of them.

For our visitors, here is some information on different modes of transportation available if you decide to combine touring with your walks. (All prices are current as of this writing and may change in the future.)

There are public buses, Tri-Met, which if boarded at the Portland International Airport takes 25 to 30 minutes for the trip to the city center and costs 85 cents.

A taxi from the airport to the city center takes about 20 minutes. The fare is approximately $20.

There is private transportation by limousine, which takes about 25 minutes to the city center. The price for the limousine is $5 for adults and $1.00 for children between the ages of 6 and 12 and free for children under 6. The limousine is operated by Raz Tranz.

The cab companies available in our city are Broadway, Deluxe Cab, New Rose City Cab, Portland Taxi Co., and Radio Cab Co. The first person pays by meter, and each additional person pays 50¢ per ride.

The bus zone fares are from 85¢ to $1.15, based on a three-zone area. For further information, call Tri-Met at 233-3511.

The major car rental companies which are available in the city are Alamo Rent A Car, American International Rent A Car, Budget Rent A Car, Dollar Rent A Car, General-Rent-A-Car, Hertz Corporation, McCullagh Leasing, National Car Rental, Pacific Coast Leasing, Snappy Car Rental, and Thrifty Car Rental.

We also have a light rail, the Metropolitan Area Express or MAX. It serves the residents of downtown, the eastside and Gresham.

The transit service in Portland is sold by time and zones. To determine the fare, count the number of zones travelled, including the zones at the beginning and end of the trip.

The Customer Assistance Office is located behind the waterfall sculpture in Pioneer Courthouse Square at 701 Southwest Sixth Avenue. The office is open from 9:00 a.m. to 5:00 p.m., Monday through Friday. A bonus for travelers in the downtown area is Fareless Square, a 300 square block area bounded by the Willamette River, Northwest Hoyt and Interstate 405 where the travel either on Tri-Met buses or Max is free.

We hope this book will prove a good adviser and friend to you, we wish you a pleasant walk and if you are a visitor, a pleasant stay and lots of happy memories of our city.

PORTLAND, HOW IT CAME TO BE

Before we get into our walks, you may want to know a few things about Portland. Perhaps just a little of our history may enable you to know us better.

Portland is, by far, the largest city in the state of Oregon. It is divided by the Willamette River, which flows in a northwesterly direction through the center of the city. The Willamette meets another river, the Columbia, several miles downstream. There the northern edge of the city begins, at the confluence of these two waterways.

When visitors come, they look at our city in awe. Here is a marvellous skyline, yet set against a background of spectacular green hills stretching for miles in a semi-circle, embracing both residential and business districts. To many, it is a beautiful and sedate city.

The downtown district, however, is becoming a lively live-in area. For those in search of a good time, Portland after dark is by no means a ghost town.

Despite some inclinations to follow a typical downtown financial "look," the inner-city has a subtle charm, with its network of intimate streets and alleyways contributing to an early Portland ambiance. There are all types of entertainment, cafes, a bistro or two, restaurants, theaters and other places where people gather to socialize.

More than 350,000 people live within the city limits, making this the center of Oregon's economic, social, scientific and cultural life.

To further enhance its significance, Portland lies in a region where an ancient Indian civilization once flourished. Records show there were inhabitants living here 10,000 years ago—the ancestors of the Multnomah Indian nation. This tribe thrived along the Willamette River. Our county was named for that famous Indian nation.

How Portland got its name has always been of interest to visitors and Portlanders, mainly because there is a fascinating story which goes with it.

Historians agree Portland was christened with the toss of a coin, a copper one no less, which resides in the collection of the Oregon Historical Society.

As the story is related, two pioneers, Francis W. Pettygrove and Asa Lovejoy, bought a claim in 1844 somewhere near what is now Southwest Front Avenue. They wanted to start a town and settle down. First they needed a name. Pettygrove wanted to name the claim after his hometown of Portland, Maine. Lovejoy, a Bostonian, was equally loyal to his native city.

They argued a bit but finally decided to settle it with a coin toss. One account had them tossing the coin under an elm tree on Front Avenue. Another had them at a "dinner party" where they decided the city would be named by the one who won two out of three tosses.

The "dinner party" sounds apocryphal, likely a tale concocted by a visiting San Franciscan. Nevertheless, Pettygrove won the toss and Portland has been our name ever since.

The city at first remained only on the west side of the Willamette River. The east side was referred to as "East Portland." It did not become part of Portland proper until years later.

The early settlers soon began developing businesses. There were produce markets, department stores and banks. In 1850 a newspaperman from San Francisco, Thomas Dryer, started a newspaper called *The Weekly Oregonian*. The paper went on to become a leading daily of the Pacific Northwest and has never ceased publishing. Today, it is one of the largest newspapers in the west.

One of the reasons Portland grew faster than its contemporaries was its link to the farming community of the Tualatin River Valley. The city was accessible to the lands to the west by a plank road. Lumber, wheat and other agricultural products were shipped over the road to Portland's waterfront and loaded onto ships embarking for San Francisco—a lucrative market then because of the "Gold Rush."

The plank road eventually became Southwest Canyon Road and Jefferson Street. There is a stone marker on Southwest Jefferson Street in the South Park Blocks commemorating that plank road.

In one of our walks, a highlight will be the Pioneer Courthouse at Southwest Fifth Avenue and Morrison Street, directly across from Pioneer Square. The courthouse was an architect's triumph, built between 1869 and 1875. To this day it is considered an outstanding example of the architecture of that period.

The square was constructed in 1984, designed by a much loved Portland architect, Willard K. Martin, who died tragically in 1985 in the crash of his Piper Cub airplane. The square has become a favorite meeting place for Portlanders of all ages. (In earlier days, Portlanders would meet "under the clock" at Meier & Frank department store diagonally across from the square.)

In another section of the central city, in the historic district, is the New Market Theater Building, 49 Southwest First Avenue. It was built in 1872 and years later became a parking garage until being totally refurbished in 1984. It now houses restaurants and offices—and is a favorite gathering place for the after-work crowd.

I should alert you to some highlights of national significance. The famous Lewis & Clark expedition made its way through here in 1805. Some contingents of that expedition reached the Pacific Coast at Seaside, Oregon. The expedition leaders, Meriwether Lewis and William Clark, were believed to the the first white men to walk through what is now downtown Portland. They even set up camp on a bluff overlooking the Willamette River. Today, the campus of the University of Portland is situated on that famous bluff.

As Portland continued to grow in the late 1800s and early 1900s, the business community looked for ways to attract more settlers. Some asked, "Why not have a celebration honoring the Centennial of the explorers, Lewis and Clark?" They did.

The Lewis & Clark Exposition, held in 1905, was so successful that the after-effects caused a population explosion from a paltry 90,246 in 1900 — to a staggering 207,000 in 1910. It dropped considerably years later, only to rise again more dramatically during the ship-building days of World War II.

At the time of the Centennial, the state's basic industries were wood products and agriculture. Today, they still dominate the economy of our state, with tourism a very close third.

Portland started changing its personality in the later 1950s and early 60s. It began, according to some observers, with construction of the period's only new high rise—the Hilton Hotel downtown. The site on which the hotel is located had been a collection of unrelated small buildings of inconsequential design.

The effort to attract the new hotel was a long-standing one. Everyone from the mayor to the governor and business leaders got into the act. When the hotel opened its doors in 1963, it was an occasion for a "big party." Everyone was invited. It was a bash that had no precedent and to this day there has not been a celebration equal to it. The fun lasted for days. During one of the "celebrity" parties, one of the celebrants carted off a prize oil painting which was part of the hotel's new collection displayed in the lobby. It was also one of the first displays of art in public places. Fortunately, the painting was later returned by an embarrassed reveler.

With the Hilton, changes began to happen. New construction started in the downtown core area. Residential high rise apartments sprang up, attracting the condo and high rent crowd. Some Portlanders were turning in their trowels and garden gloves and spending their leisure time pursuing the finer cultural benefits being offered in the city.

Attractive sculptures graced the downtown blocks. New fountains where the young and the old splashed together enhanced the homogeneity of a citizenry seeking respite from summer sun or prolonged periods of winter loneliness.

Another commercial building broke ground and soon the owners boasted its supremacy over the downtown skyline. The 41-story First Interstate Bank Tower was a bit of Los Angeles innovative architecture.

Other buildings began to make their debuts and by the late 1970s the 39-story bronze-tinted U.S. Bancorp Tower was built, breaking new ground by extending the perimeter of the downtown business district to the virtual center of the city at West Burnside and Southwest Fourth Avenue.

In 20 years, Portland had made a resounding statement with its new skyline. With that declaration came a fresh influx of new Portlanders. Today, it is not easy to find anyone who is a descendant of an early day pioneer.

With this brief history we now can measure our steps in Portland and take an easy and more appreciative walk. You will see examples of our 19th Century architecture and, at the same time, discover the new city.

One thing I insist — allow your imagination to guide you as you tour through our city. As you walk by our many shops and buildings and thoroughfares, try to acquaint yourself with our past. You may be able to imagine dusty, cobblestone streets filled with the sounds of horses and passing carriages. Listen! You may hear the whining of the sawmills along the old waterfront or even catch the scent of a fresh roasted chicken prepared by one of our early day Chinese street merchants.

Portland had romance in those days. It still has romance. You will find it in the walks through our streets and avenues and parks.

Enjoy this book. Enjoy your stay. Enjoy your walk. And if you already live here, you've got it made.

Portland Transit Mall

PORTLAND STEP-BY-STEP

How to Use This Book

The area map below shows the general area of each of the 20 walks listed in this book. Specific street locations from which each walk originates are listed at the beginning of the individual walks and can be located by using a city map of Portland for driving instructions. Check Tri-Met (see page 6) for information regarding bus transportation to the various locations.

area map

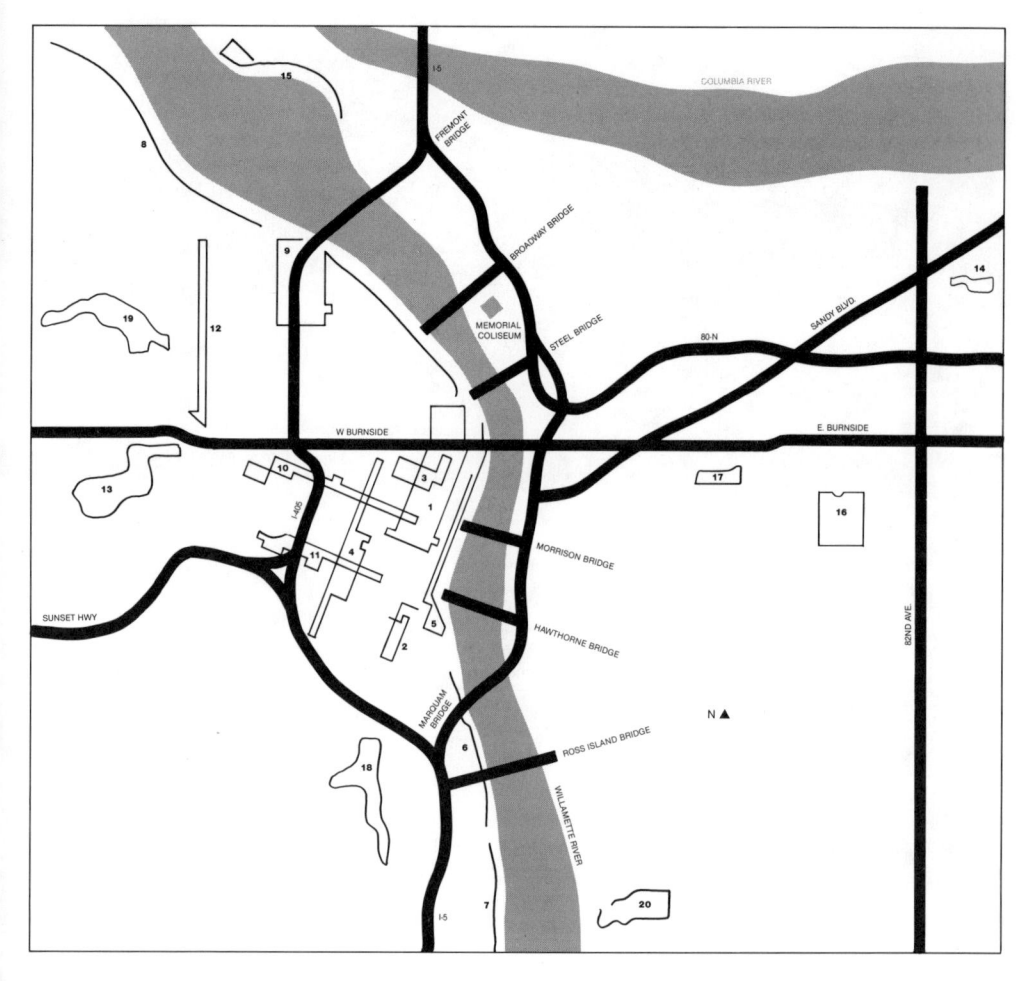

PORTLAND STEP-BY-STEP

contents

                                    Page No.

Introduction	4
Portland—Practical Information	5
Portland, How It Came To Be	6
How to Use This Book and Area Map	10

Walk No.

1	Downtown Historic Districts	12
2	Portland Center	16
3	Washington Street	20
4	South Park Blocks/Central City	24
5	Governor Tom McCall Waterfront Park	30
6	The Spaghetti Factory	34
7	John's Landing	36
8	Portland Docks	38
9	McCormick Pier	40
10	Civic Stadium	44
11	Goose Hollow	46
12	Northwest Twenty Third Avenue	50
13	Hoyt Arboretum/Washington Park	52
14	The Grotto—The National Sanctuary of Our Sorrowful Mother	56
15	Willamette Boulevard	58
16	Mt. Tabor Perimeter	62
17	Laurelhurst Park	66
18	Terwilliger Hill	70
19	Macleay Park	74
20	Crystal Springs Rhododendron Gardens/Reed College	76

1 DOWNTOWN HISTORIC DISTRICTS

Distance: 2.5 miles (4.0K)
Class A walk

A. Begin at Southwest Salmon Street and Broadway at the southwest corner of the Hilton Hotel.

If you like quaint shops, old buildings with cast iron facades, a little naughty history, a potpourri of Oriental and European delicacies, this walk offers that and a step more.

Begin in the center of the downtown business district rather than in the historic district or in Chinatown because this is where Portland began changing its personality in the late 1950s. For years, Portland was a grand old lady of the Pacific Northwest and the only excitement downtown was "cruising" Broadway on Friday nights.

It seemed then that every high schooler with a '56 Chevy was dragging Broadway, irritating the other folks who came downtown for a quiet evening at the movies or to snack at Jolly Joan's, which in the '50s was "the place," something like a cross between a Papa Aldo's and a Haagen Daz today.

One day in the '50s a representative of a leading hotel chain came to Portland, linked up with the then movers and shakers and before long this hotelman, Ford Montgomery, announced the construction of a Hilton Hotel. In those days, a Hilton Hotel had prestige written all over it. For Portland, it was the coming of the new age in downtown growth. So, it is fitting, though not obligatory, to begin our walk to the past by marking our first step at the Hilton Hotel which linked—to a degree—the past with the present.

B. Proceed east on Southwest Salmon Street.

I rather like how our early city fathers protected what in those days was the "weaker sex."

At the corner of Southwest Fourth and Salmon are the "Plaza Blocks" which comprise Chapman Square to the south and Lownsdale Square to the north. They are the blocks to the south of this intersection.

Lownsdale at one time in our history was a park habituated primarily by men. The other, Chapman, was for "Women and Children Only." Chapman was considered a safe place for women and children to lounge during walks into the central city. Men were not permitted to sit or even to walk through the square, to do so would have been a misdemeanor offense. Men stayed in their own square, quite well behaved and, during most of the days, would be seen spending their time playing cards or checkers. Incidentally, the restrictions no longer apply.

In between the two squares is a statue of an elk, which was given to the city by one of its mayors, David P. Thompson. For years there have been attempts to remove it from the center of the street (Southwest Main) but it still remains.

On Southwest Salmon, and a block east, is a neighborhood which once had inhabitants who were far from neighborly. Some of the more "wicked saloons" of Portland's post depression era lined the street. In the '30s and '40s there were a number of these tough saloons, frequented by loggers and merchant seamen. One was known as the "Bucket of Blood." No outsider dared even to walk by its doors, so the story goes, unless accompanied by "burly companions."

Nightly, the police "paddy wagon," or "Black Maria" as it was called, was summoned to the "Bucket of Blood" to cart off the "drunk and disorderly" types to the city jail. The jail was then located at Southwest Second Avenue and Oak Street and which was also the headquarters of the Portland Police Bureau. It was a nightly ritual, followed by another ritual at the Municipal Court every weekday morning.

In those days, the defendants charged with misdemeanors were gaveled "guilty" without a word uttered in their defense. It was a chapter in our history of how law and order was practiced in those days. Most Portlanders were careful to avoid these blocks whenever they came to the west side of town.

C. At Southwest Salmon and Southwest First Avenue, head north.

The Willamette Center is a three block conglomerate of buildings—principally occupied by the headquarters for Portland General Electric Company. There are many shops and restaurants in the complex, which is interest-

The Oregonian Printing Press Park

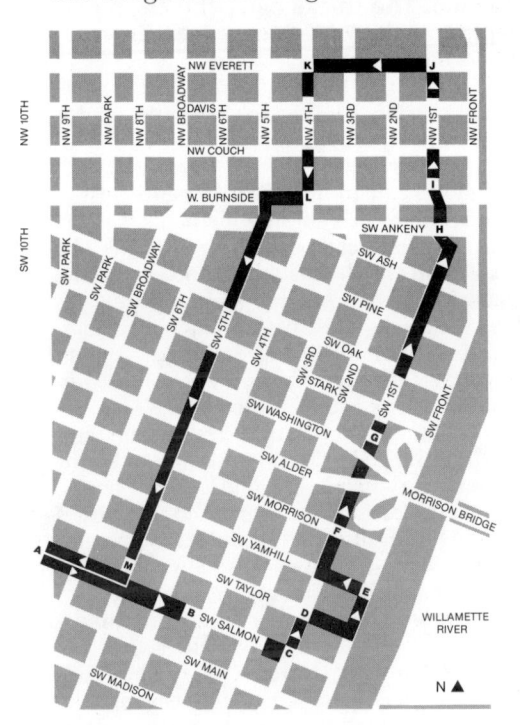

Mill Ends Park

PORTLAND STEP-BY-STEP

13

ingly designed with an elaborate network of sky bridges and escalators. The Greater Portland Convention & Visitors Association offices are here, as well as the Portland Repertory Theater company.

D. Continue north on Southwest First Avenue to Southwest Taylor, turn east one block to Front Avenue.

At Southwest Front and Taylor, at the south end of the street divider on Front Avenue, are two bollards (ship posts) which protect the "smallest park in the world."

A Portland journalist, Dick Fagan of the old *Oregon Journal* newspaper, was tired of looking at a utility pole hole every day from his office across the street. He decided to plant flowers and brighten the busy intersection. That was more than 25 years ago. The old *Oregon Journal* building, located on what is now Tom McCall Waterfront Park, is gone. Fagan died some time ago but the tiny area he planted and christened Mill Ends Park, after the column he wrote, remains. It is now an officially designated park and is maintained by the Portland Bureau of Parks.

E. Proceed north one block to Southwest Yamhill, turn west on Southwest First Avenue.

This is the east entrance to the Yamhill Marketplace building and the epicenter of the Yamhill historic district. The building was restored to its present motif during the reign of Mayor Francis Ivancie, who worked diligently with civic leaders to see that the building had a genuine sense of the past. The new marketplace was an immediate success. Not too long after it opened, the biggest bash held in the building was the victory for Bud Clark, a Portland saloon keeper who upset a "surprised" Ivancie in one of the most stunning defeats in the city's history. That was in 1984…only a year or so after Ivancie had presided over a dedication party. But that's politics.

The market has one of the finest fruit and vegetable stands in the city and, if you like "service with a smile," Gary and his staff "aim to please." There also is an exotic coffee bar offering all varieties of blends, cake and pastry shops, even a French bakery, a cheese shop, meat and fish shops and boutiques to shop further for the more personal items which are intended to enhance relationships.

F. Proceed north one block to Southwest Morrison.

This is a special place for me. At the northeast corner of the intersection is another historic site—a park somewhat larger than Fagan's but not one which has the sentiment attached to it as does the smallest park in the world. It, nevertheless, has a particularly special meaning.

Some years back a concrete structure of some curious design stood there to mark the spot of *The Oregonian* newspaper's first printing press. For years this sculpture, executed by county employees with good intent, attracted few onlookers but plenty of neglect. The historic site eventually turned into a sore spot environmentally and was on the verge of being declared a nuisance, when the newspaper decided something had to be done.

With the help of county, city and Tri-Met officials, *The Oregonian* began a quiet campaign and within a year transformed the site into an appropriate memorial. The bollards, six of them, now contain the front pages of significant news events of national and regional interest. The pages are etched in brass. There are some intriguing stories on these pages.

G. Continue north on Southwest First Avenue. The tracks carry the city's new rapid transit, MAX (Metro Area Express) of Tri-Met.

Heading north on Southwest First to Stark about one block is the Oak Street station for MAX and the beginning of the Skidmore Historic District.

Before continuing north, pause just a moment. To the west about a block was the "old" Chinese neighborhood of Portland. The restaurants in the neighborhood served the personnel of the nearby office buildings as well as the employees of the main police headquarters, then located at Southwest Second and Oak. The police building is visible from the MAX Oak Street station.

The area had not only restaurants and clothing shops but bail bondsmen, who for years earned their living, and lucrative it was, by posting bail for those arrested on charges ranging from disorderly conduct to felonies. (Today, new state laws have eliminated the need for bail bondsmen.)

However, the presence of the bail bondsmen and police station was the source for many interesting stories. One of the more interesting characters I met while covering the police beat in those days was Mickey Cohen, a flamboyant West Coast entrepreneur who had just been released from federal prison at McNeil Island in Washington after serving a sentence for tax evasion.

In the late '50s, characters like Mickey Cohen were fodder for the press. Police attempted to shield him from the media. However, luckily, one reporter managed to get an interview minutes before Cohen caught his Los Angeles-bound flight at the Portland airport.

Mickey, as he liked to be called, insisted he was "going legit" and that, upon return to his home in Beverly Hills, he had plans to open an ice cream parlor.

"It's the thing of the future," he was quoted as saying. "My ice cream is going to be the best. It's going to have lots of cream and no butterfat." And with that, Mickey made his first public statement in years and was whisked off to the waiting plane. This is a true story, all in the files of *The Oregonian*.

H. Continue north to Southwest Ankeny and First Avenue.

This is the Skidmore district and the home of the New Market Theater, which opened in 1875. Many prominent artists of the day performed there.

Although Portland in those days was primarily a logging and shipping center, it possessed a cultural strain which was fine tuned to the arts.

Unfortunately, in later years the building remained unused as a theater and for a time served as a parking garage. It was renovated in the late '70s and early '80s and today is the bright spot in the old part of town. Across from the New Market Theater building is the Skidmore Fountain, considered the first piece of commissioned art donated to the city. It was the gift of a Portland businessman, Stephen Skidmore.

I. Continue north on Southwest First Avenue. After you cross Burnside the street designation changes to northwest.

On the north side of the Burnside Bridge, the span visible just north of the New Market Theater building, is the Old Town district. Many buildings in this part of town have been restored by two Portland businessmen, Bill and Sam Naito, who turned their dream into reality as well as an asset for the community.

J. At Northwest First Avenue and Everett the distance from the Hilton Hotel is 1.25 miles. Proceed west on Northwest Everett to Northwest Fourth Avenue.

Walk along the north side of the Northwest Natural Gas building toward the "new" Chinatown. This is a traditional Chinatown district with its cluster of restaurants, Oriental motif shops and even a Chinese language school. The Chinese holiday celebrations are held in this area. However, not all the eating places are Oriental. There are some excellent Greek, Mexican and American restaurants here, but the fare is predominantly Chinese.

K. Proceed south on Northwest Fourth Avenue toward the Chinatown arched gate at Burnside Street.

L. Turn west on Burnside to Fifth Avenue at the U.S. Bancorp tower.

Southwest Fifth Avenue is part of the Tri-Met bus mall, which leads through the downtown shopping district.

M. Proceed to Southwest Salmon Street, turn west on Salmon to Southwest Broadway, the point of origin.

PORTLAND STEP-BY-STEP

2 PORTLAND CENTER

Distance: 1.2 miles (1.9K)
Class A walk

A. Begin at Southwest Fourth Avenue and Mill Street at the Church of St. Michael Archangel.

At one time the aroma of freshly baked bread, pumpernickel, rye and bagel, joined other culinary scents which identified this area as an international neighborhood. This was part of South Portland, home to young immigrant families — Jews from Poland, Turkey, Russia, Rhodes and Spain, Italians and even some Yugoslavians. Most of them are gone now. Some have died. Some moved to the suburbs when migration there was in vogue and some have even returned to occupy the high-rises which stand, self-contained and self-ventilating, on ground once occupied by their forefathers.

South Portland, or part of it, stood along this stretch of blocks. For many years this area was a refuge for immigrants who wanted freedom and a chance to make it in a country struggling to accept the newcomer. Now there are small parks and sculptured waterfalls and middle and upper class apartment dwellers enjoying the good life in the "new part of town."

I can remember such names as Colistro and Halperin, and even Mosler, who had businesses here. They were the owners of the stores (now we call them boutiques) which catered to the families who found it safe and comfortable adhering to the cuisine of the old country. While they tried to keep a hand linked to the old ways, they also struggled to adapt to the ways of their new homeland. These were times of sacrifice and of sharing and of staying together. They brought the neighborhood concept with them, they had their style of dress, cooking, and living. They were lancemen and they were paesanos.

It was the mid-'50s when I arrived. I can remember, almost as if it was yesterday, joining the queue at Mosler's Bakery on Southwest First Avenue, waiting to take home freshly baked pumpernickel which I had not tasted since my youth.

And if that wasn't enough to whet my nostalgia, I had to stop by the favorite neighborhood grocery of Colistro and Halperin, an early day odd couple who catered to the appetites of the Jews and Italians of that part of town.

In the next decade freeways obliterated neighborhoods because they no longer were able to pay their way. Many of the small single dwellings were considered too shabby and their proximity to the central city too embarrassing. Tax revenues slipped and something had to be done. These were the times when urban renewal was "all the rage" and soon 1500 people and hundreds of small businesses were relocated. More than 50 blocks were leveled and the "new town" was built.

It was all part of the big change of the '60s when, along with urban renewal, came the students setting their standards for a new morality.

Buildings of concrete and steel were erected alongside the freeways and a generation of apartment dwellers was born, abandoning their lawns and rose gardens for life in the new town.

Soon one high-rise apartment building after another took over the perimeter of downtown and a different way of living took hold in what was once single family dwellings.

It was a period of transformation. For awhile it threatened the tranquility of the hillside dwellers who feared their view of Mt. Hood would be forever obscured or lost. However, the transition was orderly and the new buildings and the accompanying architecture offered an acceptable contrast with what remained of the past.

A strong support for some of the immigrants in those days was their place of worship. For the Italians it was St. Michael Archangel Church. This was originally a chapel built for the German Catholics. In 1894 the chapel was designated for use by the nearby Italian community known as "Little Italy," a term with a derisive connotation, but used liberally in the country to identify settlements of Italian immigrants.

The church was declared an historic landmark in 1971 and today serves the downtown business community and some older residents who still come there to worship.

Ira's Fountain and Portland Towers

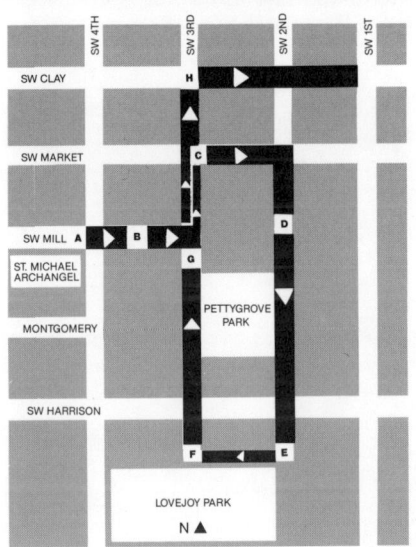

PORTLAND STEP-BY-STEP 17

B. Cross Fourth Avenue to the beginning of Portland Center.

Follow the walkway between the two buildings and then head north between the rows of young maple trees. The KOIN Tower is ahead, the Civic Auditorium is across the street and the 200 Market Building is to the right. Turn north on Southwest Third Avenue.

C. Head east on Southwest Market to Southwest Second Avenue.

This is a little tricky here but the walk is quite simple to follow. Turn right at Southwest Second and the walk continues, bordered by still another row of trees.

Rian's Atrium restaurant is to the east, or the left. The first flight of steps, six to be exact, is about 50 yards from the right turn at Second Avenue. The walk continues up a series of four flights of stairs with levels separating each flight and then ahead is Pettygrove Park.

This park was named after Francis W. Pettygrove, one of the two pioneers who flipped a coin to name Portland. The park is about an acre or less of miniature hills and hidden nooks.

The sculpture in the park is by a prominent local artist, Manuel Izquierdo. It is called "The Dreamer."

This park is perfect for picnics. On a hot summer Portland day, the residents of the nearby apartment buildings settle around the Lovejoy Fountain. The fountain was named after the other pioneer, Asa Lovejoy, who lost the coin toss.

The urban settlement has a variety of little shops and restaurants.

D. Continue south on Southwest Second Avenue.

The walk here is ideal because no vehicles are allowed. This is truly an urban park. Just south of the Lovejoy Fountain is another fountain, much smaller but offering a quieter setting.

The giant three-level sculpture named *Leland I* was placed here in 1975 and was executed by Portland artists Lee Kelly and Bonnie Bronson. It was commissioned by the Portland Development Commission and is part of the South Auditorium Urban Renewal Project. This sculpture is about ¾ of a mile from the point of the origin of this walk. The apartment towers in the park were named after US. presidents: Lincoln, Grant and Madison.

E. Turn west at Lovejoy Fountain and head to Southwest Third Avenue.

The walk here is not marked but it is the first walkway west. Harrison Street is about 50 yards to the north. One of the early highrises is the building at 255 Southwest Harrison.

F. Proceed along the west side of the Harrison Street building. Walk between the two wooden posts. Head north on the walkway.

This area also attracts downtown business employees, who come here to relax during lunch breaks.

G. Proceed north until the walk flows into Southwest Third Avenue, near the beginning of the walk.

The Civic Auditorium is on Southwest Third and Ira's Fountain is directly across the street.

The fountain was named after Portland industrialist Ira C. Keller, who was chairman of the Portland Development Commission. This, too, is a favorite gathering place. It is one of the largest fountains in the Pacific Northwest.

H. Proceed north on Southwest Third to Clay, turn east on Clay to Southwest First Avenue.

Here at this intersection is the Marriott Hotel, the Tom McCall Waterfront Park and the Alexis Hotel. This is a good crossroads point, where you can extend the walk by linking up with another one.

Orbanco Building

3 WASHINGTON STREET

Distance: 1.0 mile (1.6K)
Class A walk

A. Begin walk at Southwest Washington Street and Broadway.

Larry Hilaire was always the epitome of a restaurateur. He was in a class by himself. There was dignity and grace about this man which brought him honors, not only from his own city but from his peers nationally. He was the wizard of Washington Street when it came to culinary excellence and a man for his seasons.

Hilaire's Encore at Southwest Washington and Southwest Broadway was a landmark. His fellow restaurateurs elected him president of the National Restaurant Association and with that came added recognition.

Today, the Encore is no longer there. However, it seems there always will be a restaurant at that spot between Broadway and Sixth on Washington.

Hilaire was not the only one who contributed to the history of that street.

Let's go back to the last century and borrow a page from Terence O'Donnell's and Thomas Vaughan's book, *Portland, an Informal History and Guide.* According to the authors, at the end of what is now Washington Street was located the town's first structure, a log store which later became an inn.

But that's not all. The walk along Washington parallels Stark Street and, for those old timers and history buffs, this was the street which was the access to the Stark Street Ferry which for many years was the only way Portlanders crossed the Willamette River.

There is more: in this part of town is the oldest restaurant in the city.

In San Francisco they boast about Jack's Restaurant, the oldest in that city. It is not elegant or ornate but it does have excellent food. It is the place to "do lunch." In Portland we have Huber's. It is elegantly vintage and it hasn't changed much, or hardly any, since the turn of the century. Huber's goes back to the 1800s, 1879 to be exact.

Huber's is famous for its roast turkey, ham and other good old-fashioned American meals. Oddly, the management of Huber's has been Chinese, with the exception of the original owner, Frank Huber and immediate family. The meals have always been traditionally American because at one time Huber's was a saloon and it served ham and turkey to the beer drinking patrons. The saloon originally was owned by Huber and his cook was Jim Louie. That's how it all began.

I talked to James Louie, the son of Andrew Louie, who owns the restaurant and is the nephew of the famous Jim Louie whose photo hangs on the south wall as you enter the restaurant. The young Louie told me the same menu carrying the original recipes is still used. Of course, there have been some embellishments. The restaurant is in the Oregon Pioneer Building at 320 Southwest Stark Street. Its decor is art deco with a mahogany interior rarely seen in restaurants today.

B. Proceed east on Southwest Washington past the former Encore, now a Chinese restaurant.

The walk crosses the transit mall at Southwest Sixth Avenue and again at Southwest Fifth Avenue.

To the south on Southwest Fifth at Alder Street is the famous Meier & Frank Department Store, one of the oldest department stores in the Pacific Northwest. A son of one of the former owners, Aaron Frank, is chief of staff to Oregon U.S. Senator Mark O. Hatfield. He is Gerry Frank, who has distinguished himself with many civic accomplishments. One of these is his Konditorei in Salem, home of the "best chocolate cake in the world." He also is author of an out-of-towners guide to New York.

C. Continue east on Southwest Washington Street to Southwest Third Avenue.

Here is another famous eating and drinking place. It is between Fourth and Third Avenues, and from the outside, the entrance of Kelly's Olympian conceals an experience that is waiting inside. The name would hint at something of a lofty nature. It could be that pausing there for a spell, one could imagine achieving a more exalted feeling. Regardless of what others may say, I know several persons, a close friend or two, who have frequented Kelly's and found it rich in

Bishop's House on Southwest Stark

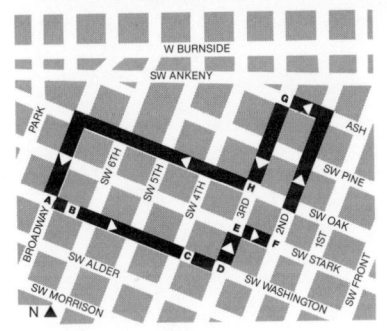

PORTLAND STEP-BY-STEP

camaraderie and other attributes which bring people together to share tales of family, love, loves lost, of jobs and of jobs lost, all stories dear to a drinking person's heart. There isn't a two-fisted drinker in Portland or thereabouts who hasn't been to, or at least been tempted to do, a night's drinking at Kelly's Olympian. It is certainly worth a peek inside.

D. Turn north on Southwest Third Avenue.

At 411 Southwest Third Avenue is one of the two entrances to Huber's. The other entrance is on Stark Street. This is an ideal place for lunch or an after-work drink. The clientele: mostly Corona lovers.

E. Turn east on Southwest Stark to Southwest Second Avenue.

At 219 Southwest Stark Street is the Bishop's House building, which was the residence for one of the city's early Catholic leaders, Archbishop Blanchet. Next door was the Cathedral of the Immaculate Conception at Southwest Third and Stark Streets. It was moved later to its present location at Northwest Eighteenth Avenue and Couch Street.

The Bishop's House has been the home also of restaurants, business offices, professional services and even early day Chinese tongs, headquartered there along with a speakeasy during the Prohibition days.

F. Proceed north on Southwest Second Avenue.

The refurbished building on Southwest Second Avenue and Oak Street was the home for many years of the Portland Police Bureau. It has been renovated and now is occupied by stockbrokers and other business enterprises.

Further north on Southwest Second Avenue at Ash Street is the heart of the Old Town District. The buildings here are an excellent example of the transitional architecture which appeared in our city during the era of the cast-iron buildings, 1851-1889, and the boom in high rise structures built in the mid-1900s.

G. Proceed on Southwest Ash Street to Southwest Third Avenue.

In this area are some small wine shops, a French bakery, newer restaurants and even another historic eating place, the Oregon Oyster House at Southwest Second and Ankeny. It never has served alcohol but is a popular spot for tourists and Portlanders who love a dash of the nautical with their meals.

H. Continue south on Southwest Third Avenue to Southwest Oak.

From here, walk west on Southwest Oak Street to Broadway and south two blocks to point of origin at Southwest Washington Street.

Lincoln Statue, South Park Blocks

4 SOUTH PARK BLOCKS / CENTRAL CITY

Distance: 2.0 miles (3.2K)
Class A walk

A. Begin at Southwest Park Avenue and Stark Street.

What I like about this walk is that Portland's past and present are there before your eyes.

Imagine, there are waterfalls in downtown Portland! There's a boulevard of giant elms and grass-covered picnic areas, as well as historical places of beauty, and, to top that, some exciting contemporary architecture.

There's more: the most famous statue in the state — PORTLANDIA. Her arrival on a flat barge on the Willamette River caused this city to go bonkers with excitement. That happened in 1986 and Portland hasn't been the same since. It's an eternal love affair.

And there is still more. This walk will allow virtually a passage in time. Portland's personality actually had its beginning in the Park Blocks, which go back to the early 1850s. At that time, the blocks were a gathering place for the townspeople and for traders who came from the nearby farms to load their goods onto seagoing vessels moored at our port on the Willamette.

The blocks in those days were nicknamed the "boulevard." It was not only a gathering point for socializing and trading but a "drag strip" for young bucks who raced their horses along the boulevard and later recounted their wins boastfully to anyone who would listen.

The area became so popular that our early city fathers decided to set it aside as a permanent series of park blocks. It was planted later with grass and with young elms which today stand along its entire length — testimony to the foresight of those early leaders.

B. Head south from O'Bryant Square on Southwest Park Avenue.

The walk begins through a series of commercial blocks which, during the business hours, have a moderate-to-heavy traffic flow. It will be only a few short blocks before coming to the dedicated, and recently redesigned, Park Blocks.

At the north end of the South Park Blocks is the Arlington Club, a gentlemen's club for the city's elite male entrepreneurs. No woman has ever been admitted to the club or even entered the club as a guest.

Diagonally from the Arlington Club is the Roosevelt Hotel. This hotel has an interesting history. It was named for "Teddy," the rough rider U.S. president. However, he never had the chance to sleep there. But another Roosevelt, also a U.S. president, Franklin Delano, did. FDR had come to Portland in the early 1930s to dedicate Bonneville Dam and Timberline Lodge on Mt. Hood and spent a night at the hotel.

Soak in more history.

This part of the blocks is where many of Oregon's rich and famous stroll on their way to the "club" and to the Arlene Schnitzer Concert Hall. The concert hall was named after one of Portland's leading patrons of the arts. Arlene Schnitzer came from a Portland mercantile family, the Directors, and married into another family of merchants, the Schnitzers, who are in steel, shipping and real estate.

As the story goes, Arlene Schnitzer, back in the late 1950s, needed something to utilize her time. She had a passion for the arts and with her husband's support opened Portland's first major art gallery. She called it The Fountain Gallery, naming it after the historic Skidmore fountain, which was a block away.

From that early start she became a leader of the arts. Through the years she championed many artists and artists' causes. Some of the leading artists in the Northwest owe in part their success to the support and encouragement of this woman. So, it came as no surprise when Portland honored her by renaming the renovated Paramount Theater the Arlene Schnitzer Concert Hall, centerpiece for the arts complex.

Across the street to the south in the new Portland Center for the Performing Arts building, is the Delores Winningstad Theater, named for the wife of C. Norman Winningstad, founder and vice chairman of Floating Point Systems, Inc., a Beaverton-based high tech industry. The Winningstads, too, have been unselfish in their contributions to the arts in Portland.

Roosevelt Statue, South Park Blocks

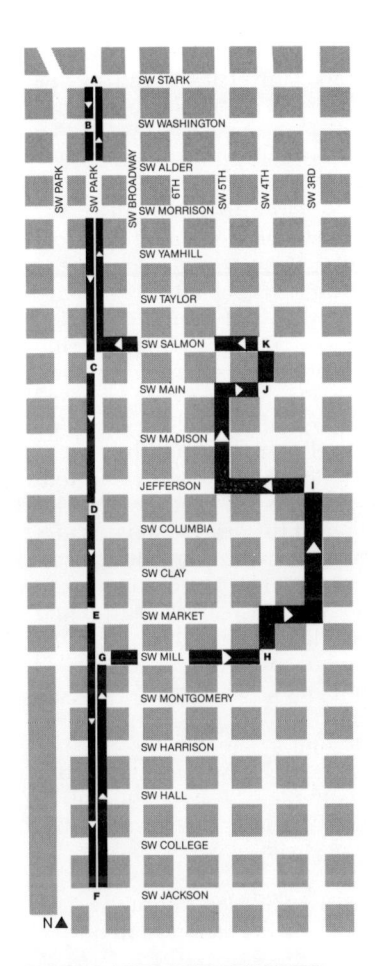

PORTLAND STEP-BY-STEP 25

C. Continue ahead.

If sculptures of famous people and interesting events are to your liking, I would suggest devoting a few minutes to examining the Shemanski Fountain in the first park block directly south of the Arlington Club. It was given to the city by the Joseph Shemanski family, also merchants who owned the Eastern Outfitting Department Store, a popular retail outlet of its day at the turn of the century.

The very next sculpture of interest, particularly for the hundreds of school children who make a seasonal pilgrimage to it, is the one of President Lincoln. It is in the blocks directly across from the Winningstad Theater. There isn't a youngster who hasn't tried to climb it and sit at his feet.

When I was a boy we had a Lincoln statue in our city. It was one of Lincoln, seated. Every year, at the anniversary of his birth, the local newspaper would try to get photographs of school kids sitting in his lap. The kids loved "Honest Abe" and were shocked everytime they read about his assassination.

The next statue in the park blocks seems to have an entirely different effect on people. It is of Teddy Roosevelt, the rough riding U.S. president, looking tough and formidable. The statue is in the next block to the south, opposite the Portland Art Museum.

When the Park Blocks were redesigned in 1986 an attempt was made to turn the statue so it faced south instead of north. I understand this wasn't the first time someone tried to turn "Teddy" around. It's been tried before but a hue and cry from Portlanders forced City Hall to leave him alone. The last time I checked, "Teddy" was still facing north, and probably will be for a long time to come.

Do some more rubber necking in this area because one of my favorite buildings is the Portland Art Museum. Among its treasures is a Northwest Indian collection, considered to be the best in the world. This is a "must" after the walk.

To the east of "Teddy" is the Oregon Historical Society, packed with mementos of Oregon history.

D. Continue ahead, southbound.

In the block between Southwest Jefferson and Southwest Columbia, in the middle (or so it appears) of the center walkway, are three huge slabs of stone. One is upright, and two seem to have been dropped, waiting to be hoisted upright. This is a sculpture in what has been designated the Peace Plaza, a spot dedicated to everlasting peace.

At first I didn't get it. I decided to stick around and watch for some people reacting. I waited only a few minutes when a mother and small child came by. The little boy, who couldn't have been older than three, tottered away from his mother and climbed onto a slab, one which was resting lengthwise on the pavement. He played for awhile and then ran back to his mother.

Seconds later, a young couple in their teens came by, stopped and sat on the slab. Suddenly the small boy reappeared, walked over to the couple, surprising them, and began playfully to pat the young woman on her knees. She returned the affection by placing an arm around the child. Looking on from a short distance was the mother. She had a smile on her face.

The sculpture seemed now to have a meaning, at least for me.

E. Continue ahead.

Portland State University began as one building transplanted from a North Portland community called Vanport. More than 45,000 people lived in Vanport until a flood in 1948 forced them all to leave, destroying property and taking lives. The city of Vanport never was rebuilt. However, the small Vanport Extention Center there was moved to what was once Lincoln High School at Southwest Market Street and Park Avenue.

I remember as a young reporter covering the talk of the president (John F. Cramer, Ph.D.) of the school which had been renamed Portland State College. The college occupied the old Lincoln High School building and a few converted offices nearby. Dr. Cramer told the gathering that one day the college would be one of the biggest in the state. Today, it vies with Oregon State University and the University of Oregon for the largest enrollment.

The school over the years has attracted outstanding scholars. One of the most interesting speakers, in my opinion, was Dr. J. Robert Oppenheimer, one of the developers of the first atomic bomb. I had the opportunity to interview him in the late '50s.

At that time, the U.S. government was conducting a series of atomic tests on the atoll of Bikini. (Yes, that's where the word for the bathing suit came from . . . a tiny island in the South Pacific.)

We were experiencing an unusually prolonged period of rain in Portland and people blamed the weather on recent atomic tests in the South Pacific islands, charging that the atmosphere was being affected by the tests and was causing the siege of inclement weather.

"Doctor," I asked him, "do you feel the recent bomb tests have caused a change in our weather pattern?" His response, hesitating only to take a puff on his pipe:

"There is more energy unleashed in one thunderstorm than there is in a hundred atomic bomb tests."

I sometimes wonder, if he were alive today, what he would say about our world and what had happened since the Bikini tests.

On a lighter note, take in some of the statues on campus. Frederick Littman's *Farewell to Orpheus* near Southwest Montgomery is another favorite gathering place, particularly during the hot summer days. To the south is a stone sculpture by another Portland artist who was a friend of Littman, Don Wilson. It is entitled *Holon* honoring Gordon Hearn, the founding dean of the PSU School of Social Work.

F. Proceed on Park Avenue to Southwest Jackson near the old grade school, Shattuck, which is now part of the University campus.

Pause here and look south and up at the hills. Visible is the famous "castle" of Portland, occupied at one time or another by some of Portland's more individualistic luminaries — writers, broadcasters and the like.

G. Now, turn back, head north on Southwest Park Avenue to Southwest Mill Street.

Walking east on Mill, pass by the historic landmark of the St. Michael's Catholic Church, built originally by the German immigrants to this country, then in later years to become an Italian National Church, the only one in Oregon.

H. Head north on Southwest Fourth Avenue to Market, turn east.

I like this part of downtown. We are often called a city of parks and here is one spot I know which receives high grades from residents and visitors, particularly during the summer months — Ira's Fountain on Southwest Third Avenue between Market and Clay. If it's a hot day, the fountain, with the highest man-made waterfall in the state, attracts hundreds. It's a perfect spot to have lunch. The Civic Auditorium is to the east of the fountain.

I. Continue north on Southwest Third Avenue to Southwest Jefferson, turn west. Turn north on Southwest Fifth Avenue.

This section of the walk goes by the vintage City Hall building, which is across from the Terry Schrunk Plaza, named after a former Portland Fire Captain who went on to become one of the city's more popular mayors.

Now comes the controversial Portland Building, designed by a leading national architect, Michael Graves. It's not modern looking but, to many, the saving grace is the statue of Portlandia at the building's main entrance on the Southwest Fifth Avenue transit mall between Southwest Madison and Main Streets. The building has been compared to an "over decorated birthday cake." Actually, it is supposed to be the first major post-modern building in the country.

Portlanders had mixed feelings about the building. However, when it comes to the "copper lady" adorning the entrance, there was nothing but praise. The sculpture by Washington, D.C., sculptor Raymond J. Kaskey, is the largest hammered copper sculpture erected since the Statue of Liberty. More than 10,000 Portlanders were on hand, cheering, as she was lowered into place on a ledge some 45 feet above the mall. She is the star attraction of downtown Portland. She was so popular that the city's daily newspaper, *The Oregonian*, ran a poetry contest and nearly 1,000 amateur and professional poets responded. There is a plaque across from the statue on which the winning "ode" is inscribed, along with a brief history of the event.

J. Proceed east on Southwest Main to Southwest Fourth Avenue, turn north.

The park across the street is Lownsdale Square, just south of its companion, Chapman Square. An interesting bit of history about the Chapman Block is that in 1924 the city passed an ordinance which made it unlawful for any man to go into the park, unless accompanied by a woman or child. Of course, the ordinance is no longer on the books.

K. Turn west on Southwest Salmon to Southwest Park Avenue.

This is the last leg of the walk and goes by the southern end of the downtown business district. The return to the starting point will mark the completion of 2.0 miles.

The walk from Salmon Street to O'Bryant Square is an ideal time to reflect on what this section could have been. At one time it was all part of the Park Blocks.

Actually, the original owner of the property had planned one continuous park to Burnside Street. Back in 1850, the owner, Daniel Lownsdale, had given the land from Southwest Jackson to Stark to the city fathers for use as a park. Unfortunately, three years after his death in 1862 his heirs sued to get the property back. They were successful only with the land between Salmon and Stark, which was returned to them. They later sold it to private investors and to this day it is still owned privately.

However, one parcel between Washington and Stark was donated years later to the city for a park honoring our first mayor, Hugh D. O'Bryant, who served from 1851 - 1852.

There is another small plot of land south of Burnside on Park which was owned by another early settler, Benjamin Stark. This parcel was donated to the city and today remains a park. It is located at Southwest Ankeny and Park Avenue.

Waterfront Park, Marquam Bridge in background

5 GOVERNOR TOM McCALL WATERFRONT PARK

Distance: 2.75 miles (4.4K)
Class A walk

A. Begin at Steel Bridge over the Willamette River at the extension of Northwest Glisan Street. Proceed south.

There are few cities our size or larger where you can go downtown, toss a line into the river and catch salmon. At one time it was unsafe to fish in this portion of the river. Whatever you caught was considered unclean because of the pollutants in the water.

When Tom McCall first came onto the Portland scene he was a journalist and television commentator for several of the local stations. From there he moved into politics, which eventually carried him to the governor's office.

His concern for the environment was legendary. Some of his critics say he went too far, causing the state to suffer financially. However, in his defense, I can say Tom McCall only reflected the attitude of his constituents at the time. It was the '60s and the topic was the environment. Yes, he told people to come visit but don't stay. However, at the time no one took him to task for saying it. In fact, they applauded the stand only to change their position when times got tough. That's all in the past now. Whatever he may have done that was unpopular was certainly overshadowed by the many achievements of his two terms in office. He used his skill with words to gain legislation which benefited the environmental well-being of the state. One of those was the cleaning up of the Willamette River.

He was proud that during his time in office he was able to make the Willamette safe again for fishing. The success got him national attention and the cities looked to Portland as an example of what could be done to clean up the rivers.

Today, it is not uncommon to see anglers either from the shoreline or their little crafts plying the waterway through downtown for the prize fish of the Northwest — the salmon.

The park has a long history of development. For many years a portion between Southwest Taylor and Yamhill streets was a large farmers' market building. In later years it became the home of one of the state's leading daily newspapers, the *Oregon Journal*. The paper ceased publication in 1985.

The building was removed when the street was relocated, allowing for a greenway which is now part of the city's park system. With the advent of the greenway other parts of the waterfront were landscaped, part of a plan which eventually is to allow pedestrians and bicyclists to travel safely from the Portland docks north of the Fremont Bridge to a point south of Willamette Park, a distance of more than 10 miles.

B. Proceed south on the walkway.

This interesting part of the city is the Historic District which includes, a few blocks from here, the Chinatown District. There are excellent restaurants in addition to some Oriental boutiques.

The glass building to the west is the headquarters of the Northwest Natural Gas Company and across the street on Southwest Second Avenue (not visible from this point) are the new offices of the Portland Chamber of Commerce.

Ahead is the span of the Burnside Street Bridge, which divides the south side of the city from the north side. Burnside is the city's longest street, stretching some 17 miles. It serves as a direct link to the Mt. Hood Highway. From downtown, it will lead directly to Gresham and the highway.

Under the bridge to the west of Northwest Front Avenue is the Jeff Morris Fire Department Museum and the home of the Saturday Market, also open on Sundays, April through Christmas. Before going further, I want to say something about Jeff Morris. He was a fireman who, in my opinion, was one of the best representatives of a city agency. He dealt effectively with the press at any level and under any conditions. He made many friends for the Portland Fire Department and this museum is a fitting tribute to him.

Let's linger here just a bit longer. At this spot where the Saturday Market sets up its stalls there stood for a number of years a lavish nightclub, the Silk and Satin. Each evening, as diners supped on delicate cuisine, a scantily-clad, red haired woman swung overhead to the sound of dinner music. She was

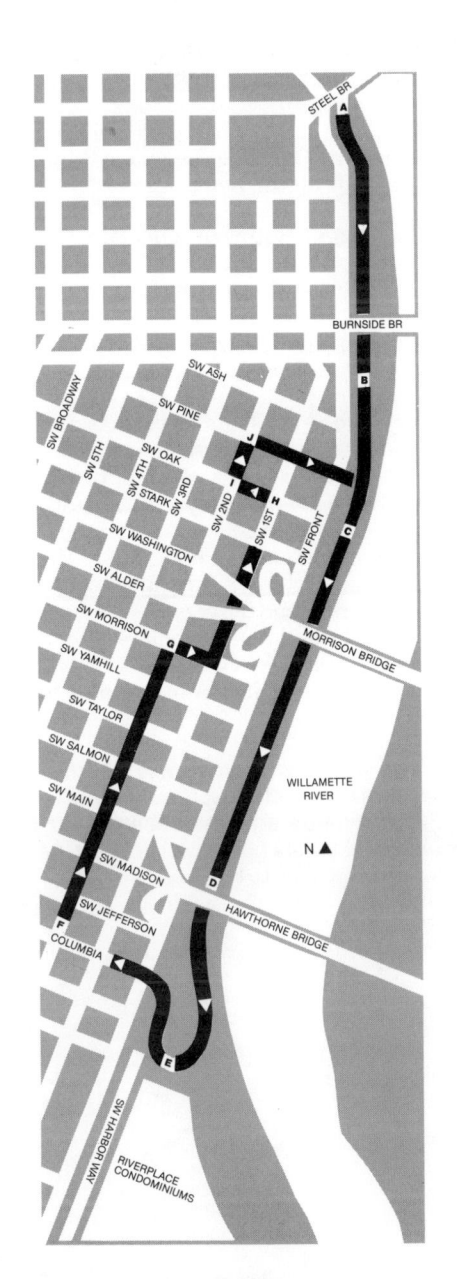

Walk from River Place to Waterfront Park

PORTLAND STEP-BY-STEP

Portland's "Girl on the Red Velvet Swing." In those days, the late '50s, such a display was considered slightly risque. It was also the appropriate place for the emerging upper class to be seen.

As the years and customs changed the restaurant slowly lost its appeal and eventually went out of business. There was an effort to revive it but a bomb blast ended that. Surprisingly, it has never been determined who placed the bomb. The blast occurred during the early morning when the nightclub was closed.

C. Continue ahead along the river walk.

Between Southwest Pine and Oak on Front Avenue, and in the park, is the foremast of the battleship *Oregon*. This is a relic of World War II patriotic sentiment (the ship itself served in the Spanish-American War). This Battleship Oregon Memorial for many years occupied a special place in the hearts of Portlanders who strolled through the downtown district. There was little to excite them in those days after the first and second World Wars and this was a memento from one of the "old" wars which at the time meant something. However, as the older buildings were renovated and new landmarks singled out, the mast has become just one of many historical objects for the curious to look at.

D. Straight ahead under the Hawthorne Street Bridge.

The seawall ends just south of here. The bollard along the railing overlooking the oval grassy beach bears an inscription and a photo engraving of the late Governor Tom McCall. This is at the extension of Southwest Jefferson Street. Ahead is the harbor of RiverPlace and the Alexis hotel, at the north end. The RiverPlace condominiums and apartments are south of the hotel.

The marina is a popular dock which offers a cluster of small attractive shops and eating places.

Here bicyclists, strollers, walkers and joggers habitat harmoniously. To provide an added touch of continental flair, the restaurants offer diners sidewalk table service. Who ever thought the Seine would come to Portland?

E. Turn west at the end of RiverPlace condominiums to Southwest Harbor Way, down to the entrance of the Alexis Hotel.

From here the walk wends its way around the oval grassy park to Southwest Front Avenue to Southwest Columbia Street.

F. Proceed west on Southwest Columbia Street to Southwest Second Avenue. Turn north on Southwest Second avenue to Southwest Morrison.

This area is now part of what used to be "a bad part of town." For years it harbored some of the least desirable characters.

G. Turn east on Southwest Morrison Street, turn north on Southwest First Avenue.

The new, distinctively designed building was completed in 1987. The Oregonian Printing Press Park is on the northeast corner.

H. Turn west on Southwest Oak Street.

Another fine eating place is McCormick and Schmick's at Southwest First Avenue and Oak Street. It is one of the better restaurants in the city and a heavy favorite for lunch. The after-five crowd is business-oriented.

I. Proceed west on Southwest Oak to Southwest Second Avenue.

The building at Southwest Second Avenue and Oak Street was for many years the headquarters of the Portland Police Bureau. It contained a city jail on the fifth floor, the Municipal Courts, the administration office of the Police Bureau and the personnel of Central Precinct. The building was renovated and entered into the historic registry. It is now an office building. The Police Bureau is now in the Justice Center.

J. Proceed north on Southwest Second Avenue, east on Southwest Pine to Southwest Front Avenue and the seawall.

From here, the walk heads north under the Burnside Street Bridge to the Steel Bridge, the point of origin.

Marina at River Place

6 THE SPAGHETTI FACTORY

Distance: 2.0 miles (3.2K)
Class A walk

A. Begin at Southeast corner of River Place, which is off Southwest Front Avenue and Montgomery Street.

It all began on Southwest Park Avenue in downtown Portland, in a restaurant where they catered to the West Coast version of Damon Runyon, Meyer Berger and Red Smith, famous national newspaper by-lines of the 1930s and 1940s.

In those years, the Virginia Cafe, 725 Southwest Park Avenue, was the place to "do lunch" for another collection of colorful local newspaper characters. Two of them were L.H. Gregory, who for 50 years covered sports for *The Oregonian*, and Ben Hur Lampman, the paper's Poet Laureate of Oregon, whose editorial writings made early morning coffee a mellowing intermission before the day's chores began. They always reserved a table in the small dining area on the balcony, above the booths, and ordered the clam chowder. The Virginia Cafe made noteworthy Manhattan and New England chowder.

They were greeted by a member of the Dussin family, early Greek settlers who came to Portland with a talent for creating successful restaurants. From their beginning, the Dussins went on to become some of Portland's more successful entrepreneurs. As time went by, members of that early Portland family moved on to other restaurants, opening the Iron Horse on Southwest Broadway across from the Hilton Hotel, then to the Union Station and finally the big leap: The opening of the Old Spaghetti Factory at Southwest First Avenue and Pine Street.

Eventually the company expanded to other states. However, the showpiece of the family is the Old Spaghetti Factory at 0715 Southwest Bancroft. The restaurant, overlooking the Willamette River, hardly deserves the name "factory." It has the appearance of a lordly estate, while still preserving the magic that made the "old" Old Spaghetti Factory a favorite for family dining.

B. Proceed south along River Place Road and head toward the river.

At the south end of the boat moorage is RiverPlace rowing shop, the home of Portland's crewing enthusiasts. The sport has really caught on in Portland.

In the early morning, before the river traffic takes over, the shells are in the river, rowing north almost to the Fremont Bridge and south toward John's Landing.

The voice of the coxswain calling the rhythm for the strokes of the oars is sometimes the only early morning sound except for the distant groans of an occasional freight train crossing the Steel Bridge.

C. Head past the Newport Bay restaurant on the pier, turn south.

The path from RiverPlace property leads to a narrow dirt path which runs east of the Pacific Power & Light steam plant. The large vacant field will be developed soon, according to city planners. The high rises to the west are the condos and rental buildings of the South Auditorium Urban Development Project.

D. Proceed along field, around gate, and veer right under the Marquam Bridge, then south on Southwest Moody.

There are no signs here to indicate the name of the street, but directly across the street to the south of the Marquam Bridge, which is overhead, were the temporary offices of the Lake Oswego-bound double deck electric railcar.

E. Continue south on Southwest Moody.

To the left, or east side of the street, are old warehouses, including an old steel company building. Most of the industrial activity in this area will be gone if the city proceeds with its revitalization program. The neighborhood will eventually be made up of commercial buildings with some housing planned south of the Ross Island Bridge. This is the span south of the Marquam Bridge.

F. Proceed ahead to Southwest Bancroft, which is unmarked but is one block south of Southwest Lowell.

The Spaghetti Factory is to the left on Southwest Bancroft, overlooking the Willamette River.

G. Return to the place of origin via the same route.

Old Spaghetti Factory

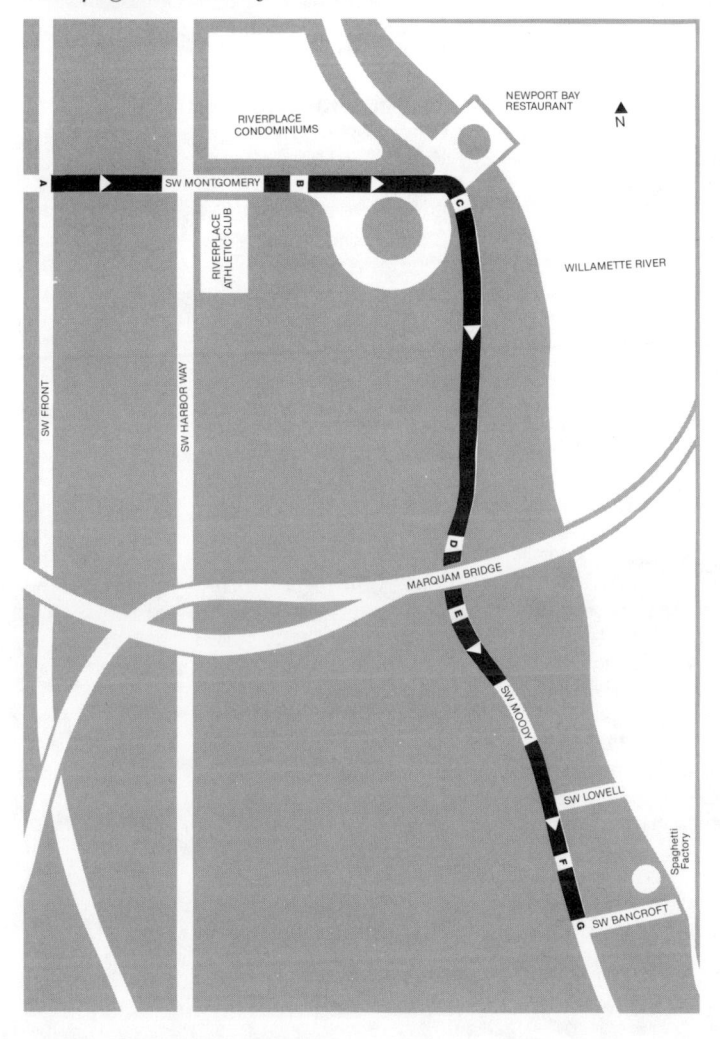

PORTLAND STEP-BY-STEP 35

7 JOHN'S LANDING

Distance: 3.7 miles (5.9K)
Class A walk

A. Begin at Southwest Bancroft Street on Southwest Moody Avenue, one block east of Macadam Avenue.

For decades our river remained hidden by industrial plants, wrecking yards, salvage depots and wire fences. It was a river many Portlanders saw only when they crossed our bridges. We were denied the chance to enjoy the fulfilling qualities of a beautiful urban waterway.

Despite this denial, Portlanders maintained a romantic loyalty and hoped that one day the industrial barriers would be gone.

Soon it all began to happen. What had been obstructing our view for years seemed to just go away when the preservation of our environment became part of our freedom in the 1960s.

We started to turn our river banks into greenways and parks for the enjoyment of the many rather than into more industrial depots for the benefit of a few.

Industrial leaders saw that times were changing and began to care. They realized what the river meant to the welfare of all the people of the city.

Just south of downtown in the part of South Portland on the highway leading to Lake Oswego, changes took place. For years this neighborhood was culturally apart from the mainstream. It was thought of as only a "link" between the downtown and the higher priced residential districts to the south in Dunthorpe and Lake Oswego. It was also known as "Furniture Row" because the street southwest of Macadam Avenue was the location for many furniture manufacturers.

The furniture industry on Macadam Avenue began with a German craftsman, Bruno Paul John. He arrived in Portland in 1898, worked hard and by 1928 had merged a number of plants into the B.P. John Furniture Company. This industry flourished for many years.

After the heyday of furniture making faded, others came with different ideas for developing the neighborhood, realizing its importance because of its closeness to the river. They brought a new direction, a future few dreamed ever would come true. Changes began to occur. A group of Portland investors was formed, chaired by John D. Gray, an industrialist with a reputation for getting things done. Included in the group were some descendants of B.P. John.

That was in the late 1960s. With the excitement of change in the air, Gray dedicated his energies to a new concept for living on our river. In a few years, what was once a drab waterfront became a charming blend of shops, restaurants, condos and boat docks. It was named John's Landing, an enduring salute to an enterprising German immigrant.

B. Proceed south along railroad tracks to the River Forum Building, about two short blocks.

This is a new building hugging the Willamette River bank. Take the path at the north end of the building and follow it toward the river and then south.

This is part of the Willamette Greenway, which was mentioned in other walks in this book.

C. Straight ahead, follow the path.

The area has restaurants on the river as well as commercial buildings and condominiums. (The path leads through a restaurant parking lot and eventually along the east side of the new condos.)

There are newer units at this end of the complex. The other units are part of the original design and are quite luxurious, with expansive views of the river.

D. Follow path to end of condo area to the Willamette Sailing Club.

The sailing club marks the beginning of Willamette Park, which is owned and operated by the City of Portland.

The park is a favorite for picnickers and those who love to sail. The facility for the boat ramp was developed in cooperation with the State of Oregon Marine Board, the U.S. Department of Interior, the Bureau of Outdoor Recreation, the Department of Housing and Urban Development and the Corbett-Terwilliger-Lair Hill Planning Committee.

PORTLAND STEP-BY-STEP

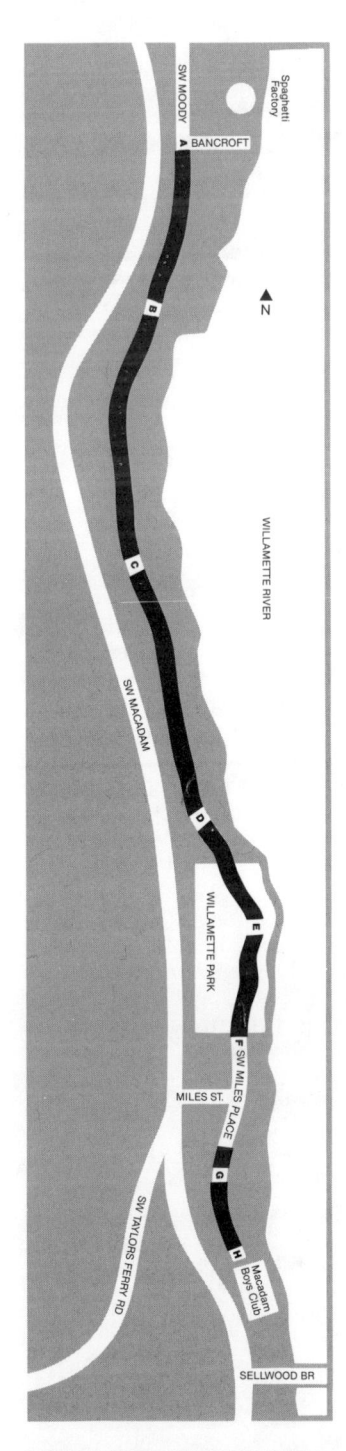

This is all part of what's known as Metropolitan Water Group.

E. Take winding path through park.

This foot path winds interestingly along the waterfront and a bluff which overlooks the southward view of the Willamette River. A small river colony of homes, a rather unusual location, is to the south of the park and can be partially seen from the bluff. The Sellwood Bridge is in the distance, to the south. Across the river from this point is Oaks Park, one of the oldest amusement parks in the state.

F. Proceed from park path through a low metal gate barrier to Southwest Miles Place and Southwest Miles Street, which intersects Southwest Macadam Avenue above to the right and west.

Here are about 25 small river homes.

G. Proceed ahead to wooded area.

The path winds gradually down to the Macadam Bay Club, whose address is 7720 Southwest Macadam Avenue.

The club's parking lot is the turnaround.

H. Return to point of origin at Southwest Bancroft and Moody.

John's Landing landmark at 5331 Southwest Macadam

PORTLAND STEP-BY-STEP

8 PORTLAND DOCKS

Distance: 5.0 miles (8.0K)
Class A walk

A. Begin walk at Northwest Front Avenue and Northwest Fourteenth Avenue.

This is a walk which should be taken, but only on a weekend.

This is the industrial belt of Portland but, despite that, there is a charm in this part of town which has no equal anywhere in the city.

Many years ago this was the site of the Lewis & Clark Centennial Exposition commemorating the 100th anniversary of the arrival in the Oregon Territory of Meriwether Lewis and William Clark.

The Exposition was staged in 1905 around Guilds Lake, a shallow body of water on the west branch of the Willamette River. The event attracted hundreds of thousands to the exposition grounds, once the homestead of Peter Guild, a pioneer rancher who migrated here in 1847.

The northwest hills offered a beautiful, natural background for the show and for years afterwards Portlanders spoke with pride about the success of the Lewis & Clark Exposition of 1905.

When the fair closed and the last remaining building was dismantled, the city began dumping, pouring and pumping fill into the shallow lake so the spot could be utilized as a place of commerce. By 1911 the first lot was platted and the future of the area was established.

Today the lake is gone and in its place is one of the Pacific Northwest's most thriving transportation and shipping centers.

Trucks, rail cars and ships converge here, bringing products from as far away as Asia and carrying goods from our farms and forests to many foreign and domestic markets.

On the weekend there is a lull broken by an occasional freighter or barge easing its way to our port or by a freight train passing through to its final destination.

It is during the quiet time of the weekend when walking the deserted street from the Fremont Bridge north some 2.5 miles that the drama which takes place during the week really can be understood.

It is the sight of the huge warehouses, the freighters moored at the terminals holding patiently for cargo and the caravan of tractor trailers waiting to be mobilized for still another journey which gives this part of our city an awesome vitality.

B. Ahead on Northwest Front Avenue.

Stay on the sidewalk on the east side of the street. It will lead to the turnaround point of the walk.

The hills of Forest Park are to the west in the background and partially visible from this point.

About 0.8 of a mile brings the walk to Terminal 2. A ship can frequently be seen at this terminal.

C. Continue ahead on Northwest Front Avenue.

At 1.5 miles into the walk the four lanes of Front Avenue converge into a 2-lane road.

The area here affords a good view of the rail lines, the main route for trains heading north to Seattle and east to Spokane, Washington, the tip of northern Idaho, Montana and finally Chicago.

At the 2.0 mile mark there is a better view of Forest Park, which is 8 miles long and the largest park within the official boundaries of any city in the U.S.

D. Continue ahead.

The Lamp Post Steel Company is the point for turning back. This is 2.6 miles from the point of origin.

The small bridge to the left leads to Highway 30 which goes to Astoria. This highway is known by many names, one of them the Columbia River Highway. Actually, it is one of the first transcontinental highways leading from the east to Astoria. It is known in the east as the Lincoln Highway.

Beyond this point are the Zidell Construction Company and oil tank storage facilities. In the distance is the St. Johns Bridge, considered one of the more attractive suspension bridges of its kind in the west.

E. Return to point of origin.

Willamette River west of Broadway Bridge

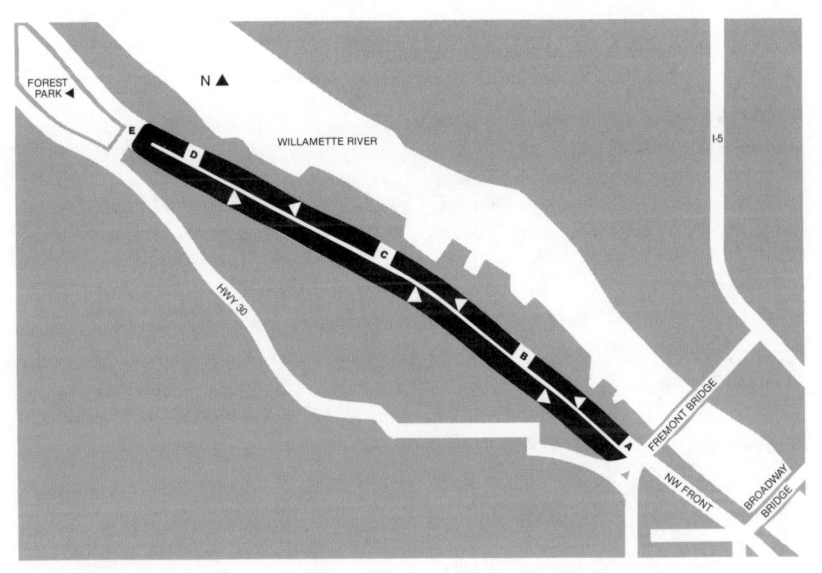

PORTLAND STEP-BY-STEP

9 McCORMICK PIER

Distance: 3.25 miles (5.2K)
Class A walk

A. Begin walk at north end of the Steel Bridge at McCormick Pier near moorage.

For years, Portlanders either ignored or resented this part of town. It was too industrial. Too old. Too ethnic. Whatever the reason, only the oldtime residents and young loyalists held allegiance to this end of Northwest Portland.

However, in the late '60s changes began here as elsewhere. Young people discovered the neighborhood and moved into the small, Victorian-style single-family homes. Prices also were reasonable. A home in the Willamette Heights, nearby, in the late '50s and early '60s could be yours for under $20,000 and even $15,000. Makes you want to cry, doesn't it?

When the new residents moved into these small homes, they poured love and energy and what money they had into brightening the neighborhood. It was not "The Heights" but it was the next best thing.

In conjunction with these individual efforts, on the other side of the tracks in the heavy industrial zone another dream was coming true.

Not too far from the Union Station, in fact, across the street to the east, two young men saw a potential in a warehouse and abandoned river bank cluttered with debris and relic of past businesses. For years a warehouse, a wharf and a feedmill were squeezed between two early 1900s bridges: the Steel Bridge to the south and the Broadway Bridge to the north.

Sam and Bill Naito sparked a renaissance of rebuilding that is still going on. In addition to restoring the usefulness of the buildings in Old Town, they ventured to build Portland's first multi-unit riverview apartments.

The choruses of doubting Thomases chirped as expected but the Naitos moved ahead, and today nearly 300 single family units occupy one of the more exciting spots on the Willamette River. It is also scenic from the standpoint that, although there are the vibrations from trains, the sounds of MAX and the mix of recreational and commercial traffic, there is a beauty about it all which begins when everything is quiet in the early morning and the first heron can be seen winging gracefully overhead in search of a piling to perch on. That signals the opening of a new day on this part of the Willamette. This is the view from McCormick Pier, the dream the Naitos made come true.

The apartments have been ideal for those young executive types who love to walk instead of drive to their offices in nearby downtown. And, if it is cold and miserably wet, the convenient "MAX" only a few blocks away in Chinatown is boarded free of charge. For this is the beginning of Fareless Square and a great way to start the day.

Some day soon, I'm told, the empty Albers feed mill on the north side of the Broadway Bridge will undergo a change and, instead of being an interim warehouse for the Naitos, may turn into something livable and cozy.

There is more to the walk which, just beyond the midpoint, goes by one of Portland's favorite mini-breweries, offering a delightful and refreshing pause.

B. Begin either on the river's edge walk which is on the McCormick Pier property or on Northwest Front Avenue. Head north.

If it's a lovely day, the river walk is preferred. The sternwheeler *Columbia Sightseer* may be moored just north of the Steel Bridge. It is there from autumn to late spring and then during the summer it moves to its home moorage in Cascade Locks, upstream in the Columbia River. Directly across from the McCormick moorage is a feed mill loading dock. Freighters from other world ports come here, generally to load grain which is shipped in by rail from the Columbia Basin.

Nearby is the Thunderbird Motel, the first of the chain which eventually grew and amassed a fortune for its founders, Tod McClaskey and Ed Pietz. The glass structure is the Memorial Coliseum, dedicated as a lasting memorial to the state's war dead. It has recreational and exhibit facilities.

C. Straight ahead to the Broadway Bridge.

At the end of the McCormick Pier walkway is a good vantage point looking northwest.

McCormick Pier and Union Station

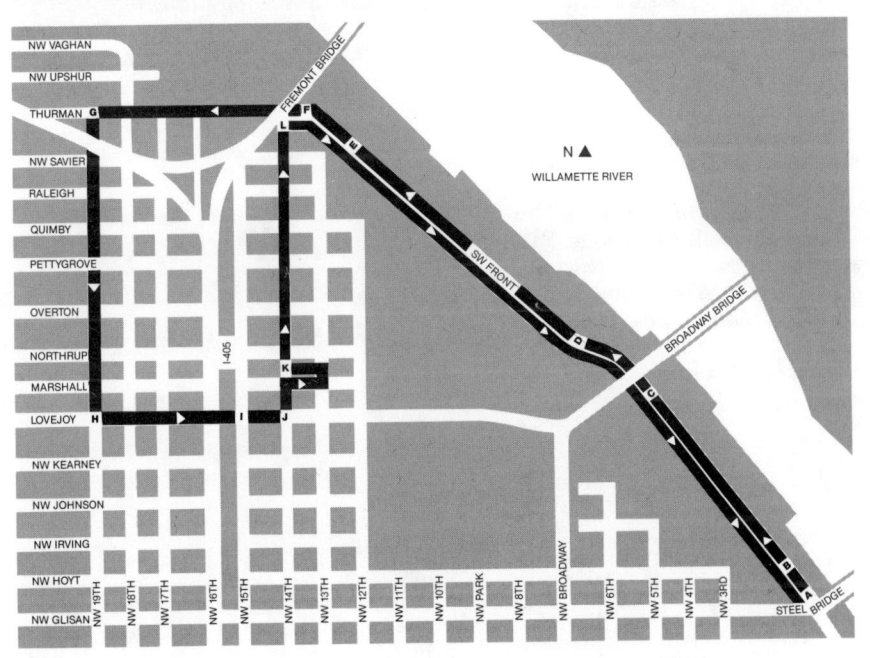

PORTLAND STEP-BY-STEP

Here the river widens and is the spot where the tugs turn the big ships around and point them for the open sea some 80 miles downriver.

D. Turn left off the walk toward Northwest Front Avenue.

If the gate facing the Fremont Bridge is closed, turn south and at the end of the fence near the parking structure is an exit which is opened during the daylight hours. Upon exiting, turn right and head for the Fremont Bridge, a mile from the Broadway Bridge which is directly overhead.

E. Straight ahead to the Fremont Bridge.

The building at the north side of the Broadway Bridge is the old Albers feed mill. Farther ahead down the street is the parking lot for the River Queen restaurant, a converted sternwheeler offering dining on the river. Still ahead is the new business complex called Fremont Place, a combination of warehouse and business offices. This is a plus for this part of the city. The builders, the Pendergast Company, provided a passage soon to be linked with the greenway. This marks another step in the proposed river walk which will be more than 10 miles long, accommodating bicyclists, walkers, joggers and the casual stroller.

F. At the north side of the Fremont Bridge cross Northwest Front Avenue and the railroad tracks to Northwest 14th Avenue. Continue west on Northwest Thurman Street.

Here is a little pocket of mixed cultures. At 1701 Northwest Thurman is the site of an old neighborhood tavern, LeFebvre. It served the mill workers and metal workers who lived in the area. It was a favorite drinking hole. This was a strong Yugoslavian neighborhood. Part of this area was known as "slabtown" because the home owners stacked the winter supply of wood in front of their homes. From this neighborhood also came two of the country's top baseball players: Johnny Pesky and Mickey Lolich. Some family members still live in the vicinity.

Farther up the street is the popular men's and women's outfitters, Norm Thompson, a store of national reputation.

G. Turn south on Northwest 19th Avenue under the ramps of the Fremont Bridge.

The church at the corner of Northwest Thurman and Savier Streets is St. Patrick's, dedicated March 16, 1890, in honor of the Irish saint.

Next door to the church is the mission of San Juan Marcias, the Hispanic vicarate for the Catholic church.

H. Proceed south on Northwest 19th Avenue to Northwest Lovejoy. The Careunit Hospital of Portland is at that intersection.

This is part-industrial, part-commercial and part-residential. Take some extra time and see the brownstone row houses on Northwest Irving between Northwest 18th Avenue and Northwest 17th Avenue. They are worth the detour.

I. Stay on Northwest Lovejoy to Northwest 14th Avenue.

Getting thirsty? This area has several micro-breweries which serve drinks over the counter.

J. Turn left on Northwest 14th Avenue to Northwest Marshall Street.

You're getting closer. At Marshall Street turn right to Northwest 13th Avenue. The Bridgeport Brewery has its hours posted on the door. The brewery conducts mini-tours.

K. Return to Northwest 14th Avenue. Straight ahead to the railroad tracks.

Now, back to the point of origin.

L. Cross Northwest Front Avenue and head east to the Steel Bridge.

Statue in Pioneer Square

PORTLAND STEP-BY-STEP

10 CIVIC STADIUM

Distance: 2.7 miles (4.3K)
Class B walk

A. Begin at Southwest Morrison Street and Southwest First Avenue at One Financial Center building.

A section of Southwest Morrison Street was known as the "Miracle Mile" for many years. That was between Southwest Broadway and Tenth Avenue. And every morning at Southwest Tenth Avenue and Morrison Street the parade began: the dowdy ones and the dignified ones, the wealthy, the wealthier and the wealthiest, the in-betweens and the poor ones. Manning's Restaurant was their morning mecca. Here they found their tables and laid claim to them for years. Groups developed, self-contained social circles that grew as the years passed.

Then one day Manning's closed and with it only the memory was left of the merchants and the professionals and the politicians and the assorted others who gave this corner eatery a distinctive personality.

No longer would the Zell brothers come in and have coffee alongside the LaGrands, or Dave Singer, or the Schumachers.

No longer would Vic Atiyeh, the young state legislator, come in from the family store, a third generation business in fine rugs, to have his usual Saturday morning breakfast.

A new generation of building began which saw a parking lot turned into a center stage, a public square where people parked themselves and not their cars

Morrison Street became a renewed street, part of it closed for almost two years to make room for MAX, the light rail.

There is a bubbling fountain now in the block known as Pioneer Square.

It's exciting again to walk on Morrison Street between Meier & Frank and Nordstrom's and see this architectural beauty which devoured a parking lot. Once it was the site of the Portland Hotel, a grand edifice which stood for years, and was dignified to the end. Now people come to the square to clamor for attention, or sit, or stare. A few play and some have lunch and enjoy the show.

There's much more interesting history on this street and it will lead to Portland Heights, one of the older bastions of culture in the city.

B. Straight ahead on Southwest Morrison from Southwest First Avenue, head west.

The new glass structure (One Financial Center) was built by Pendergast and Associates, the same company which put together the designer warehouse and office buiding called Fremont Place on Northwest Front Avenue near the Fremont Bridge.

At one time this portion of Southwest Morrison Street was cluttered and neglected. That has changed. New buildings, renovated buildings and even sidewalk sculptures farther west between Southwest Fifth and Sixth Avenues have glamorized the street.

C. Ahead on Southwest Morrison Street to Southwest Fifth Avenue.

However, from Southwest Third to Fifth there will be new high rises and new department stores in an area which has been idle for years. Construction begins in 1988 and by the 1990s all will be completed.

D. Straight ahead on Southwest Morrison Street to Southwest Eleventh Avenue.

Here is a slight jog off Morrison Street to take in a cluster of buildings built by some of the city's fraternal organizations.

E. Turn north on Southwest Eleventh Avenue to Southwest Alder Street.

The walk goes by the old Elks building on the east side of Eleventh Avenue. This also has been the home in the 1950s of the Columbia Athletic Club, which lasted a few years. Today the building is the home of the Princeton Athletic Club.

F. Proceed west on Southwest Alder Street to Southwest Thirteenth Avenue.

The First Presbyterian Church at Southwest Alder Street and Southwest Twelfth Avenue was organized in 1854, about five years before Oregon became a state.

G. Proceed south on Southwest Thirteenth Avenue and west on Southwest Morrison Street.

Another old timer is the Neighbors of Woodcraft building, erected in 1928. This is at Southwest Fourteenth Avenue and Morrison.

H. Ahead on Southwest Morrison Street to Southwest Fifteenth Avenue.

Here is the home of the Scottish Rite of Freemasonry and, directly across from it, the Masonic Center. The Masonic Center building was formerly the Portland Elks Lodge headquarters, now at 4121 Northeast Halsey Street.

I. Straight ahead past the Civic Stadium to Southwest Twentieth Avenue and Morrison. Turn left (south) uphill.

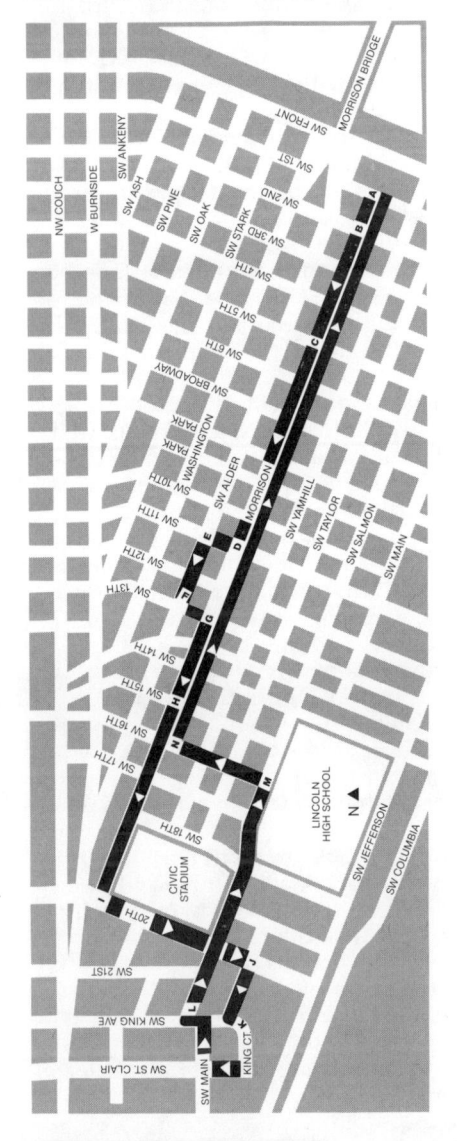

The Portland Towers is at the top of the hill — an early upscale residence and one of the city's first urban apartment high rises. The Multnomah Athletic Club is to the east of the intersection at Twentieth Avenue and Salmon Street. The club is the largest facility of its kind in the state and a popular social and business gathering place.

J. Straight ahead on Southwest Twentieth Avenue to Southwest Main Street.

This is the lower portion of Portland Heights and at one time was the neighborhood of Portland's old families.

K. Turn right on Southwest Main Street to Southwest King Avenue, turn left on Southwest King Avenue to Southwest Kings Court, which is a short, narrow street. Go one block, to Southwest St. Clair, turn right at Southwest Main Street, turn left onto Southwest King Avenue, left to Southwest Salmon about 50 feet, turn right.

In this cluster of older homes, more of the early mansion types, lived the Harvey Dicks, Elizabeth Gauld and the Corbetts, a few of the early families who gave Portland a cultural base in the early 1900s.

L. Proceed downhill on Southwest Salmon Street.

To the ladies of the Heights, the polite activity took place at the women's Town Club at 2115 Southwest Salmon Street, where membership was selective. The club is still active but membership is declining.

M. Proceed past Multnomah Athletic Club, past Lincoln High School to Southwest Sixteenth Avenue, turn left or north to Southwest Taylor Street.

Between Southwest Sixteenth and Seventeenth Avenues on Taylor is the printing facility of the Oregonian Publishing Company. The newspaper's business and editorial offices are at 1320 Southwest Broadway.

N. Proceed north to Southwest Morrison Street on Southwest Sixteenth Avenue, turn right (east) and return to point of origin at Southwest First Avenue.

PORTLAND STEP-BY-STEP

45

11 GOOSE HOLLOW

Distance: 1.5 miles (2.4K)
Class B walk

A. Begin at Southwest Fifth Avenue and Southwest Jefferson Street.

Goose Hollow. To some Portlanders the name means a tavern at the bottom of the hill where literary types, architects, politicians and others of lesser persuasion meet to make having a glass of beer a social event.

For years the neighborhood has been the location of a famous tavern which became even more noteworthy when its owner, Bud Clark, challenged the incumbent mayor, reportedly unbeatable, to a contest at the polls. The result: a stunning defeat for the incumbent. The tavern owner slipped one over on the mayor, the press and the pollsters and smiled all the way to City Hall. The result has been interesting for Portlanders. More importantly, it has added more recognition to Goose Hollow and, more pointedly, to the tavern, still owned by the Clark family.

The tavern sits across the street from the homestead of two early Portland pioneers, Thomas and Minerva Carter, whose farm was a gathering place for migrating geese. This was back in the mid 1850s. As time passed, newer settlers to the area simply called the Carter homestead "Goose Hollow" because it was below the hillside where the geese gathered while resting on their migratory trips.

In later years Goose Hollow became a quiet residential pocket in the southwest side, a convenient place to live for those who wanted to be close to the central city and still have a quick access to one of the largest public preserves in the city — Washington Park.

But there is more to this neighborhood which snuggles at the foot of Portland Heights. There is the historic Kamm House which some years ago was turned into an elegant restaurant by an interior decorator, Eric Ladd, who wanted to give Portland a class restaurant. He did. Unfortunately, it did not survive. The house stood empty for almost a decade until it was sold and renovated into offices and apartments.

When Bud Clark moved into the neighborhood, it was to relocate his tavern, from South Portland to its present location on Southwest Jefferson near Nineteenth Avenue. The neighborhood was again in the spotlight.

B. Proceed west on Southwest Jefferson Street.

The area leading to Goose Hollow is a social mixture ranging from the steel and glass PacWest Building on Southwest Sixth and Jefferson to older homes and apartments. The University Club, founded in 1897 with present quarters built in 1913, is one of the most distinctive buildings on the walk. It is located on Southwest Sixth and Jefferson just west of the PacWest Building.

Across the street to the north on Jefferson is *The Oregonian* building where the newspaper's news and business departments are located.

C. Straight ahead on Southwest Jefferson Street.

The walk intersects another walk mentioned in this book, the South Park Blocks.

D. Stay on Southwest Jefferson.

Crossing the freeway, looking north, Mt. St. Helens, the volcano, can be seen on a clear day. The volcano is in Washington, about 40 miles north of Portland.

The tall building in the distance to the right is the Terminal Sales Building, located on Southwest Morrison between Southwest Twelfth and Thirteenth Avenues.

E. Straight ahead.

Now, the walk begins to descend into the Goose Hollow district. KGW-TV and radio and KINK radio are on the north side of Jefferson. The upper level of Lincoln High School can be seen to the rear of KGW.

F. Ahead on Southwest Jefferson Street, cross Southwest Sixteenth Avenue.

The large building with semi-cylindrical shaped roof, rust colored, is the Multnomah Athletic Club and the brick structure to the left is the parking garage for the club. In the background, northwest of the club, are some of the prestige midtown apartment buildings tucked neatly along the east perimeter of Portland Heights.

The Old Church

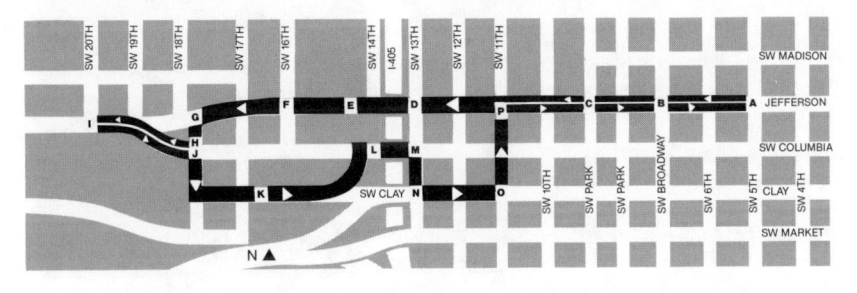

PORTLAND STEP-BY-STEP

G. Straight ahead to Southwest Eighteenth Avenue and Jefferson Street.

Two blocks ahead on the right is the Goose Hollow Inn.

H. Turn south to Southwest Columbia and Eighteenth Avenue. Turn right, head west past the United Methodist Church.

The inn is now quite visible. It should have an awning with an imprint of a goose. The inn was one of the first public drinking and eating estblishments to ban smoking (one day a week), a bold and courageous step at the time.

I. Ahead west on Southwest Columbia to Southwest Twentieth Avenue, turn left.

Here are some of the remains of the carriage days of Portland. The first structures are the cast columns and walls of an old Portland home, restored partially by Eric Ladd, the designer and decorator. There is part of the Lincoln House at the fir tree. Near the tree and in what was a foundation, embedded in the south side is a stone slab on which is inscribed "The Morning Oregonian." This came from the newspaper's former home at Southwest Sixth Avenue and Alder Street, downtown. It was taken to this spot as part of a plan for a larger structure which did not materialize.

The finished building is the Kamm House at 1425 Southwest Twentieth Avenue, built by Captain Kamm, a Portland sea captain. It was originally restored by Eric Ladd, who turned it into the Kamm House restaurant.

About 50 feet from the Kamm House looking east, is the downtown skyline, showing First Interstate Bank Tower, the tip of the Portland Towers apartment building and the upper floors of the KOIN-TV Tower. To the north is the bronze tinted building of the U.S. Bancorp.

J. Return to Southwest Columbia, turn right toward Southwest Eighteenth Avenue. Turn right on Southwest Eighteenth Avenue to Southwest Clay Street, then head east.

In this area to the south, and worthy of intimate exploration, are some of the older, less tidy residences of Goose Hollow near the underpass.

K. Stay on Southwest Clay Street.

The tall concrete structure is one of the first new high-rises in Goose Hollow.

The small Victorian style homes have been renovated in the past few years, significantly adding to the charm of the neighborhood.

L. Ahead to Southwest Fourteenth Avenue, turn left or north one block to Southwest Columbia, turn east, cross freeway.

Here is another opportunity to see the volcano. This is one of the best vantage points in the mid-town area, on a clear day, of course.

M. Turn right at Southwest Thirteenth Avenue to Southwest Clay on the east side of the freeway.

N. Ahead on Southwest Clay Street to Southwest Twelfth Avenue.

The Grace Bible Church is at the corner. It was built in 1911.

O. Ahead on Southwest Clay to Southwest Eleventh Avenue.

This is the famous Old Church, built in 1882. It was the Calvary Presbyterian Church and it was later restored by private contribution and the U.S. Department of Interior. It is on the National Registry of Historic Places.

This is the end of the walk. I felt it would be relaxing, particularly if it is summertime, to visit the Old Church, sit in the pews and take in the organ music. At noon, there are sack lunch recitals and everyone is welcomed.

P. To return to the origin of walk, head north two blocks to Southwest Jefferson Street, turn right to Southwest Fifth Avenue.

Looking north on Northwest Twenty Third Avenue

PORTLAND STEP-BY-STEP

12 NORTHWEST TWENTY THIRD AVENUE

Distance: 1.8 miles (2.9K)
Class A walk

A. Begin at Henry Thiele restaurant at Northwest Westover, just west of Northwest Twenty Third Avenue at West Burnside Street.

Henry Thiele restaurant has been in this neighborhood for a long time. It was here when Ray Milland was playing amorous roles with Claudette Colbert, both names faintly recognizable to anyone under 40.

Although the restaurant is not considered a part of the Twenty Third Avenue lifestyle, it does have significance. It is a sort of beacon that guides people to this part of town. It has been here since the art deco period of the 20s. However, it was a newcomer to the block, Rose's, which really started things moving. This newcomer eventually attracted others and soon an ordinary thoroughfare turned into a street of multiple personalities.

When Rose Naftalin first opened her restaurant in 1955, it was rare to find anyone who had ever heard of a bagel. So, what did Rose bring to Twenty Third Avenue? Not only bagels but cheese blintzes, gefilte fish and hot corn beef and pastrami sandwiches, on rye no less, plus giant multi-layer chocolate cakes and mammoth cinnamon rolls. The menu became the talk of Twenty Third Avenue and soon every sweet tooth in the entire city came to experience the unusual pastries at Rose's.

Rose went on to become a legend in her own time. She even wrote a book, *Sinfully Delicious*, published by Random House, which told the world about the little lady on Twenty Third Avenue who turned a predominantly goyim neighborhood into the Northwest's "Lexington Avenue."

What Rose Naftalin had started in the early 50s as a young entrepreneur from Toledo, Ohio, has become an avenue of places to do lunch, to do shopping and to do buying of things out of the ordinary. Northwest Twenty Third Avenue has no equal of its kind in the city.

Today, walk by the opened kitchen door of Rose's or drool in front of the deli case at Paul Bergen's for a hint of what lies ahead.

B. Proceed north to Northwest Everett, turn right to Northwest Twenty Third Avenue.

At this intersection is the Everett Market building, for many years a laundromat until early in the 1980s when things began to change on this corner.

Enjoy the market which offers enough delights to make the stay here almost a vacation. I particularly like the produce stand where everything from an Arkansas black beauty apple to some of the lesser known greens such as limestone lettuce, fennel and Swiss chard can be found.

C. Turn north on Northwest Twenty Third Avenue.

Rose's is on the west side of the street just north of the parking lot on Everett. Now begins the series of fine eating places and carefully situated boutiques.

For years the blocks ahead were lined with small professional offices, older apartment houses, a movie theater (now gone) and a 24-hour restaurant which served freshly baked pies and pastries. There were many convenient outlets which served the neighborhood. In other words, it was a typical street of small merchants catering to the basic needs of the nearby residents.

When changes began in the 60s and 70s and into the 80s the personality on the street attracted shoppers from other sections of the city.

D. Continue north on Northwest Twenty Third Avenue at Irving.

Irving Pharmacy has been here for many years and can be a fun place to shop for more than pharmaceutical items. Ask for "Milt." Tell him, "Joe sent me."

E. Ahead to Northwest Lovejoy.

The Good Samaritan Hospital and Medical Center is one of the key industries in this area and one which contributes significantly to the local economy.

The Esquire movie house at Northwest Kearney and Twenty Third Avenue closed its doors after many years of bringing good movies.

In this pocket are restaurants, service stores and other shops which defer to discriminating tastes.

F. Continue to Northwest Savier and Northwest Twenty Third Avenue.

At this intersection is a neighborhood "landmark," Besaw's, which reopened this year under new ownership and after being closed since 1972.

Years back, Besaw's tavern had a reputation for bean soup, roast beef and smoked ham sandwiches. Its reputation reached far into the city. Unfortunately, the white collar types were never able to do lunch because Clyde Besaw opened at 2 p.m. Some say he did this to discourage "those types" from frequenting his place, which he felt better served the locals.

Fortunately, I lived in the neighborhood and was able to enjoy occasionally the culinary skills of Mr. Besaw.

Farther ahead to Northwest Thurman are Harris Wine Cellars and other retail shops.

G. Return to point of origin.

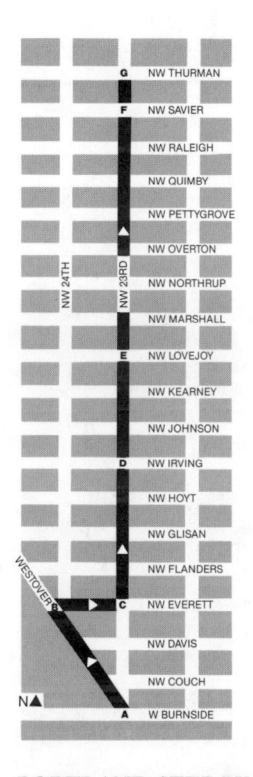

PORTLAND STEP-BY-STEP

13 HOYT ARBORETUM/ WASHINGTON PARK

Distance: 5.4 miles, not including side tours (8.6K)
Class C walk

A. Begin at Southwest Vista Avenue and West Burnside Street.

I had some misgivings about this walk because it is more than a walk, it is a memory.

It begins with a frenzy at an intersection in Portland that is a crossroads of many different social cultures. There are restaurants and food stores here, real estate offices and boutiques, candy stores, drug stores, beauty salons and flower shops.

Many years ago this intersection was sedate. The Cotillion for the young women of Portland Heights was presented each year in a grand Victorian-style building at the intersection of West Burnside and Twenty Third Avenue, on the spot where a realtor now conducts sales.

The future matrons of Portland's business leaders danced here, properly attired and trimmed in white gloves. It was the heyday of the debutante.

Today, this intersection, which is at the bottom of a hill, is the center of an expanding business community.

From early morning to early evening there is a homogeneous flow of the blue collar, the white collar and the fur collar. Some off to work in the open air of the shipping docks. Some off to work in the cloisters of the high rises. Some off to their rewards for years of work and dutiful partnerships.

It is a pattern of our way, in our life, in our time and in our country.

While it may sound hectic to some, it translates into something few of us ever give ourselves enough time to think about. That there is freedom in all this frenzy.

When I thought about doing the walk, I knew it would mean more than a little history, or passing by homes of nicer neighborhoods, or walking through another one of our parks extolling the beauty of the ponderosa, the fir and the sequoia or calling attention to a nest of black-capped chickadees or pointing to what is feeding on the dandelions.

To get the full benefit of the walk, which is to say to get more than health benefits, it should be taken when the staging is at its best.

Because of the distance and the gradual but steady climb, pick a day when autumn or early spring is in the air. A weekday would be ideal because of the contrast from the opening of the walk to its conclusion. Pick one of our favorite days when either a light mist or a rain makes the outdoors an undeniable experience.

Then, begin a passage through Portland's main attraction which takes in our International Rose Test Gardens, our zoo, our Forestry Center, the Hoyt Arboretum and finally, a war veterans' monument, a memorial that must be seen to be understood.

This will mark the high point of the walk. Let's begin.

B. Proceed west up the south side of West Burnside Street from Southwest Vista Avenue, which is directly across from Northwest Twenty Third Avenue.

The climb here is steady and the view is obstructed by the natural high terrain on either side of West Burnside Street. This part of the walk—about one-half mile—is in a heavy traffic zone.

C. Proceed to the flight of four steps, turn left onto Southwest Tichner Drive.

Continue uphill. This is about a 6% grade and begins to level off at the intersection.

D. At Southwest Tichner Drive and Southwest Kingston Avenue turn right on Southwest Kingston Avenue.

A small colony of homes in this part of Kings Heights borders the northwest end of Washington Park, which is several blocks from this point.

E. Proceed on Southwest Kingston Drive to Southwest Parkside Drive at stop sign and turn right onto Southwest Fairview Boulevard.

This begins a second climb. However, it is not as difficult as the opener. I thought the Burnside and Tichner hills the most difficult of the walk.

This is still Kings Heights and many of the homes here have excellent views of the city.

International Rose Test Gardens

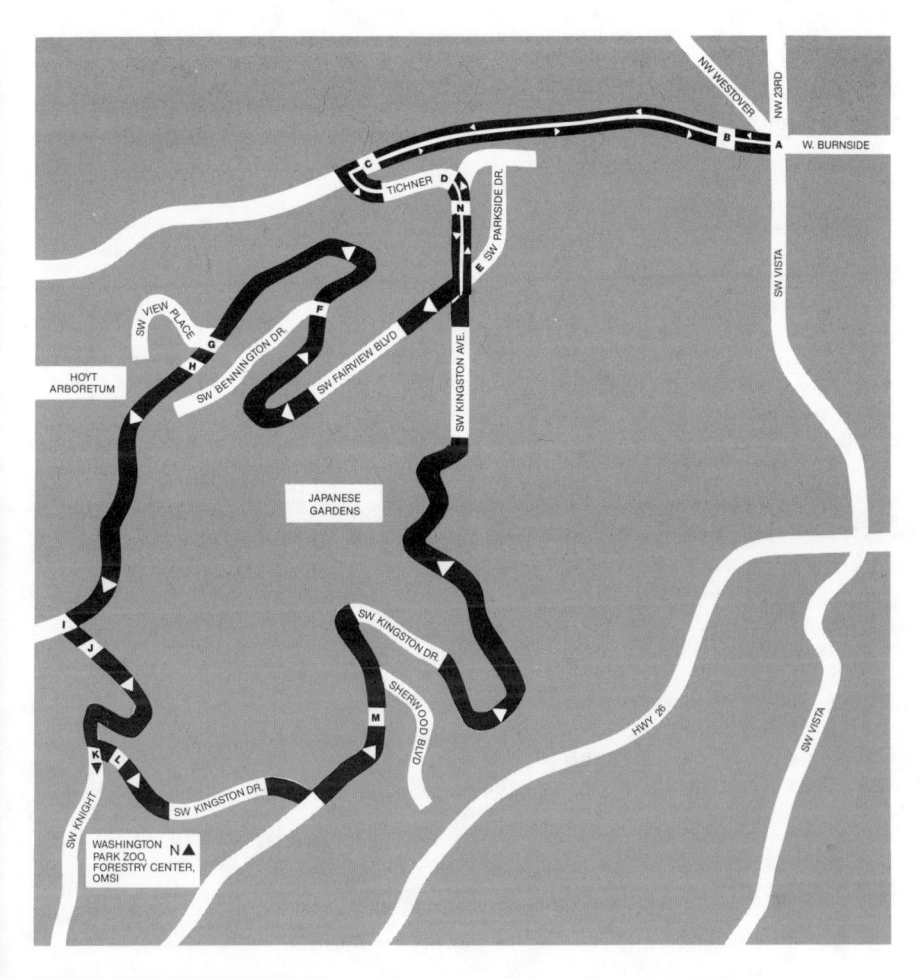

PORTLAND STEP-BY-STEP

53

F. Stay on Southwest Fairview Boulevard. It is winding. Cross Southwest Bennington which is about 1.8 miles from starting point. Continue on Southwest Fairview Boulevard.

The street continues to curve.

This area is heavy with residential homes in the middle-to-upper-middle bracket.

G. At Southwest View Place and Southwest Fairview Avenue there should be a sign "Sharp Curves." Stay on Southwest Fairview.

Now, the entrance to Hoyt Arboretum is near. There is a stop sign on top of the hill which is the entrance to the arboretum, a collection of trees and trails covering some 200 acres.

There is a visitor center, called the "Tree House" at the beginning of the Oak Trail which leads into a portion of the arboretum. The visitor center is open between 10 a.m. and 4 p.m., Mondays through Sundays, depending on the availability of the volunteer staff.

This will make a good detour but is not calculated in the mileage for the walk.

There are blue spruces, dogwoods, firs, hemlocks, holly and even Himalyan pines among many other species in this park.

An interesting sight about a quarter mile off Southwest Fairview Avenue is a tall Douglas fir with a gash on the south side of its trunk. A sign on the tree says it was struck by lightning April 15, 1982. The gash runs from near the base of the Douglas fir almost to the top. It is a hideous laceration which transmits a frightening picture of what happened on that April day.

Deeper into the arboretum there is a view of the city and also the city of Vancouver in Washington. Mt. St. Helens is visible on a clear day.

H. Proceed south and continue to walk on Southwest Fairview Avenue.

The area across from the visitor's center is a sheltered picnic area which is in another section of the arboretum.

I. Ahead on Southwest Fairview Boulevard to Southwest Knight Boulevard.

From the arboretum area to the turn on Knight Boulevard is about one mile.

J. Turn left onto Southwest Knight Boulevard.

This leads deeper into Washington Park and the conglomerate of tourist attractions such as the World Forestry Center, the Zoological Gardens, the Rose Gardens and the Oregon Museum of Science and Industry. The latter will be moving in the early 1990s to a new location on the Willamette River in the central city.

K. Continue on Southwest Knight Boulevard to Zoo, Forestry Center and OMSI.

We can detour here to explore this area.

There is an intermission in our walk, a point of reflection which begins behind the World Forestry Center. It is a detour covering only one quarter of a mile but is is worth taking.

It begins on a pathway into what has been named a "Garden of Solace," a memorial to U.S. servicemen from Oregon who died in the Vietnam War and to those still missing.

The path leads onto a spiraling ascending walk. Suddenly there is a reminder of the explosive 60s when a war brought a threatening division of opinion in our country. Somehow, this monument heals any division that still may exist.

It's hard to imagine the power of this memorial.

There are, along this quarter-mile, five semicircular black and gray stone alcoves. Etched in granite are the names of those 751 Oregonians killed in action.

The first alcove, a station of reflections, begins with the names of 25 Oregon men killed between 1959-65. Above those names, incised into the granite, are events which took place concurrently in Oregon during those years. Each alcove covers a certain period of the war ending with the years 1972-76 when nine servicemen lost their lives.

Then, in the distance, far from the granite markers and at the highest point of the memorial, is the last alcove. There are 40 more names carved in the granite, representing a final resting place for those Oregon Vietnam veterans listed as missing in action.

To their loved ones they finally have come home.

L. Return to Southwest Kingston Drive after a visit to the Forestry Center and the other attractions.

Walk alongside the road, facing traffic. It is downhill part of the way There is some level terrain. There are more views of the city on this final leg of the walk which will continue for another two miles.

M. Continue to Southwest Sherwood Boulevard and Southwest Kingston Drive.
Pass the tennis courts.
A detour just to the east of the courts, down a flight of steps, is the entrance to the International Rose Test Gardens.

N. To stay on the walk, continue north on Southwest Kingston Drive to Southwest Tichner Drive.
Return down the hill to the four steps, turn east on West Burnside Street to the point of origin.

Viet Nam War Memorial

14 THE GROTTO
The National Sanctuary of Our Sorrowful Mother

Distance: 1 mile of Grotto trails (1.6K)
Class A walk

A. Begin at Southeast 82nd Avenue and Sandy Boulevard.

I found this to be a short walk, but when it was over, what I saw will remain with me perhaps all of my life.

I didn't believe it could be as beautiful as they said it was.

"Hardly," I thought. "Not up there on 82nd and Sandy."

I knew that area. It is heavily traveled with commercial and passenger vehicles, some frantically racing to catch a plane at the nearby Portland International Airport.

What could be so beautiful in a part of the city which was so hectic? For years the strip (and the name seemed appropriate) harbored marginal motels of questionable reputation.

That has changed. However, Sandy is still far from a tree-lined boulevard where one envisions casual Sunday strollers. There must have been a reason to locate this calm spot, The Grotto, amid all this frenzy.

B. Proceed east from Southeast 82nd Avenue and Sandy Boulevard to Grotto entrance at Southeast 85th Avenue and Sandy Boulevard.

As I began my walk into the Grotto, my mood changed. My worries and anxiety seemed to go away. Perhaps it was the image of the suffering depicted in the "Stations of the Cross" which made me forget my pain. It was worth the visit and the walk.

C. Follow the path toward the main Grotto.

This is an ideal place to be during hot weather because the fir trees, which dominate the Grotto, provide quite a bit of shade.

D. At the 7th Station of the Cross there is an incline, a turn, and the path climbs slightly and levels off.

In the open area, or the main Grotto, masses are said outdoors from May to September. During inclement weather, the masses are in the nearby chapel.

The gift shop sells tokens for the elevator, which goes to the upper level of the Grotto. Here, the Servite Order of priests and brothers have their monastery where they handle all the operational business of the Grotto.

The story of this beautiful shrine, which has been a tourist attraction for many years, began before the turn of the century. I was told that a young priest by the name of Ambrose M. Mayer came to the Pacific Northwest as one of the area's first Servite parish pastors. He saw this spot which, at the time, was owned by a railroad and was for sale. The area had a sheer granite cliff and other natural attributes ideal for a sanctuary, something he had vowed to build since his youth.

The name Grotto stems from the cave, 30 feet wide, 30 feet deep and more than 50 feet in height, which is in the rock wall and now houses the Grotto altar. The cave, cut into the side of the cliff, rises more than 150 feet above the lower level of the grounds. A carrara marble replica of the famous *Pieta* of Michelangelo above the altar is the focal point of the outdoor cathedral.

E. Take elevator to left of cave. Go straight ahead from the upper level elevator exit.

There are trails on the upper level which pass through the Margaret M. Casey Peace Garden. This sanctuary is dedicated also to a "Vision of Peace." There are other religious statues and works of art throughout this level which have a quieting effect.

There is about one-half mile of trails on this level, equal to the trails on the lower level.

The Grotto has become a part of Portland since its construction in 1924. For all these years, the men of the Servite Order and the Missionary Sisters of Our Sorrowful Mother have made this a "Vision of Peace" and solitude for everybody to enjoy.

And the community outside the Grotto has shown its gratitude, exemplified by such business leaders as John Elorriaga, retired chairman of U.S. Bancorp, and Harry Merlo, chairman of the board and chief executive officer of Louisiana-Pacific.

These two men and others led a capital fund drive, raising $1.75 million toward a $4 million campaign for revitalization and renewal of the grounds. It was their way of thanking the Servite Order for bringing the Grotto to Portland.

The Grotto

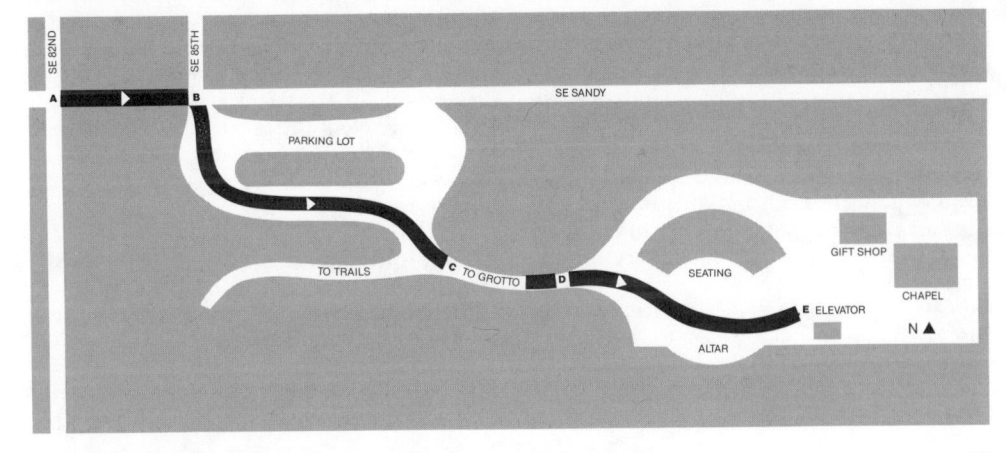

15 WILLAMETTE BOULEVARD

**Distance: 1.5 miles, one way (2.4K)
Class A walk**

A. Begin at North Portland Boulevard and North Willamette Boulevard.

When Henry Kaiser came to Portland, he came to build ships for the country.

It was early in the 1940s. Labor was scarce. The able-bodied were off fighting the war in Europe and in the South Pacific. The German forces had moved swiftly through western Europe and were threatening the shores of the British Isles. The Japanese had stunned the ill-prepared Allied forces in the Pacific.

Americans needed Liberty ships to hasten supplies of men and materials to bolster weakened defenses on two fronts.

Kaiser came and he provided. He did so with a labor force drawn from the bleak open spaces of the Dakota badlands to the inner ghettos of broiling Chicago slums.

He wanted workers, all kinds, and all kinds came: from tall, broad-chested males with flat feet who had failed the Army's physical to war widows and single young women. These latter eventually became cast as "Rosie the Riveter," symbol of a nation united in a struggle.

All through the day and through the night a work force of thousands toiled on Swan Island. This pancake of land had been converted from a one-time hope for a beautiful city park to a massive industrial hub producing almost a ship a week for the Allied forces.

Swan Island became a strategic center, a vital link in the nation's military buildup. It was a stunning transformation from what had been an airport serving the City of Portland to a massive ship building factory on the Willamette River.

Years earlier, before World War II, Swan Island had been dedicated as Portland's Municipal Airport. That was in the Fall of 1927. At that time, it was considered an ideal location for an air terminal for the future.

Such early aviation greats as Charles Lindbergh and Tex Rankin, a famous stunt flyer, landed at Portland Municipal Airport at Swan Island.

However, in the late 1930s Portland began searching for another site suitable to the needs of a growing aviation industry. It was during this period that Mayor Joseph Carson of Portland envisioned Swan Island as a permanent city park.

Mocks Bottom, the area adjacent to the island, was to be reclaimed and developed into a beautiful recreation center. There was to be tennis, basketball, football, baseball, and all forms of sports on the 253-acre island.

But his predecessor, the colorful George L. Baker, had a different idea.

"Let me tell you something, mister!" he said in an interview with a writer for the Sunday *Oregonian*. "If we don't land some industries for Portland we won't need parks. Portland needs industries." Baker was on target. That was in January, 1936. A few years later Kaiser came to Swan Island.

Today, the island viewed from Waud's Bluff at the eastern tip of the University of Portland campus is an industrial and commercial complex. This is hardly what Lewis and Clark would have envisioned when they ventured to this point, the farthest distance they traveled on the Willamette River on April 3, 1806.

In one full sweep, Swan Island, the Willamette River winding its way through the center of the city and the neighboring hillsides are framed. If it is a clear day, Mt. St. Helens, the volcano, and Mt. Hood are visible.

B. Proceed west off North Portland Boulevard onto North Willamette Boulevard.

This is a middle to upper middle income neighborhood of homes, situated on a bluff which actually overlooks Mocks Bottom and Swan Island. The sidewalk, unfortunately, is on one side of the street at a point farthest from the edge of the bluff. The view here is mostly of the city at a distance and the superstructure of ships under repair at the Swan Island docks.

C. Straight ahead on North Willamette Boulevard to entrance of University of Portland, between North Fiske Avenue and North Haven Street.

The university was founded in 1901 by Archbishop Alexander Cristy, who headed the Roman Catholic Archdiocese of Portland.

Swan Island Docks and downtown Portland from North Portland

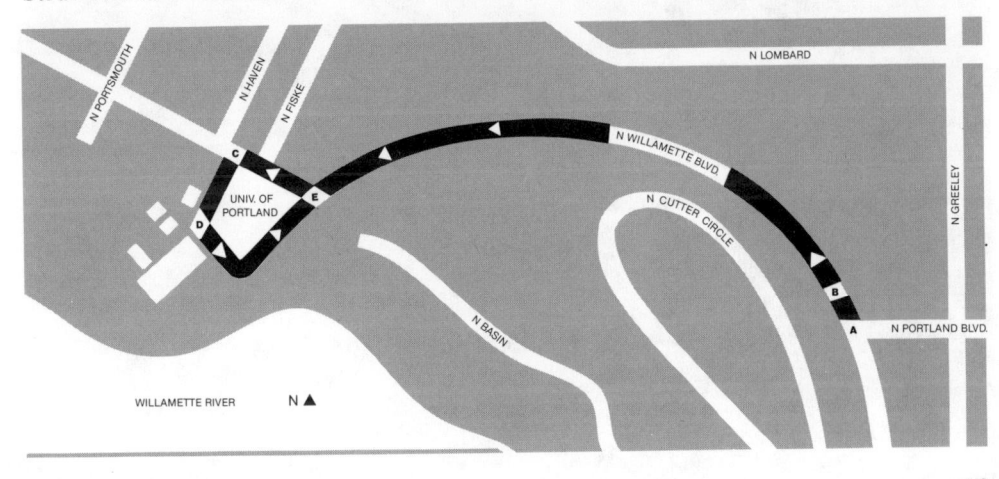

PORTLAND STEP-BY-STEP

The property was purchased from the Methodist Episcopal Church. It started as Columbia Prep, then was changed to Columbia University and finally to the University of Portland. When the Methodists ran the school, it was called Portland University.

In 1902 the archbishop invited the teachers of the Holy Cross Order from Notre Dame to staff the school.

Today, there are 2,800 students on campus, which covers 92 acres in North Portland.

The oldest building, built in 1891, is still standing. It is West Hall. The most recent addition to the campus is the chapel of Christ the Teacher, designed by Pietro Belluschi, an architect of national reputation.

D. Proceed down main entrance to Buckley Hall, turn left and head to farthest point in parking lot.

The Lewis and Clark marker is on a large boulder. This is the spot for the grand view of Portland.

E. Continue to follow the road left to the exit which is North Willamette Boulevard.

Return to point of origin.

Lewis & Clark marker

Mt. Hood from Mt. Tabor

16 MT. TABOR PERIMETER

Distance: 2.7 miles (4.3K)
Class B walk

A. Begin walk at Southeast Sixtieth Avenue and Lincoln Street.

It was hard for me to think of Mt. Tabor as a special park, as different from others in our city.

So, what if it had an extinct volcano? Granted, no other parks in Portland have a volcano as a drawing card, but when I first heard about Mt. Tabor, I could not imagine getting excited about peering into the plugged up throat of a volcano that died thousands of years ago.

My curiosity, of course, got the better of me and I went there with my wife and our two young children. I stood and looked at the cinder walls of what was at one time the cone of the volcano. I felt absolutely nothing.

It looked like a natural amphitheater carved out of cinders. There were picnic tables, a storage area and it was all rather unassuming, not the least bit threatening.

We ate our lunch, played some, chased around, got tired and went home. It was a pleasant and typical Sunday afternoon.

"Well, what did you think of it?" I asked my wife.

"Of what?"

"The Mt. Tabor volcano," I countered.

"It's interesting.... Did you bring in the picnic basket?"

That was the last time I ever thought about Mt. Tabor until some years later.

It was a quiet Sunday. My life had changed considerably since that day many years ago when I visited the cinder cone at Mt. Tabor.

I was heading toward the neighborhood grocer to purchase some milk that I had forgotten the day before. A friend waved me down. He appeared frantic.

"Did you hear? It's all over the radio," he said.

At 8:31 a.m., Sunday, May 18, 1980, Mt. St. Helens, the mountain which my kids said reminded them of an ice cream cone, erupted, creating a fiery avalanche which maimed, killed or destroyed practically everything within a 25-mile radius. It was one of the worst disasters of our time. Nothing of such deadly force had ever struck the Pacific Northwest. While thousands watched safely from miles away, there was fear among those who lived in the shadow of nearby mountains such as Mt. Hood.

It was then I learned that our Cascade Range was part of the "Ring of Fire" — a chain of volcanic peaks that ring the Pacific Ocean from South America through Canada and Alaska to Japan and beyond.

Soon, we began wondering about Mt. Hood and Mt. Baker and others. Mt. Lassen in northern California, where the last recorded eruption in the United Stated took place on May 22, 1915, was also on our mind.

Could the reactivation of Mt. St. Helens ignite others in the Pacific Northwest? There were still gas emitting fumeroles on Mt. Hood and Mt. Baker. However, Mt. Tabor had been quiet for thousands of years.

When I returned to Mt. Tabor recently, after an absence of many years, I read the marker again, this time with much more interest. The words describing the eruption had more meaning to me. They were not just words etched on a marker to designate an historic occurence back before recorded time.

Somehow, the picnic tables and amphitheater seemed so out of place.

B. Proceed north on Southeast Sixtieth Avenue from Southeast Lincoln to Southeast Salmon Street.

The road will lead to the interior of the park. It will be a steady upward climb to the cinder amphitheater, also known as the Volcanic Theater.

There are many ideal viewpoints in the park, excellent for picnics. The roads are open certain hours for vehicle traffic. There will also be joggers and bicyclists during the daylight hours. They have discovered the hills of Mt. Tabor quite challenging.

The discovery that Mt. Tabor had been a volcano was made in 1912, years after it became a public park. It was during grading operations in the park that crews digging into the site discovered large deposits of volcanic cinders.

C. If the detour on Southeast Salmon has not been taken, continue north on Southeast Sixtieth Avenue to Yamhill.

PORTLAND STEP-BY-STEP

Amphitheater, Mt. Tabor

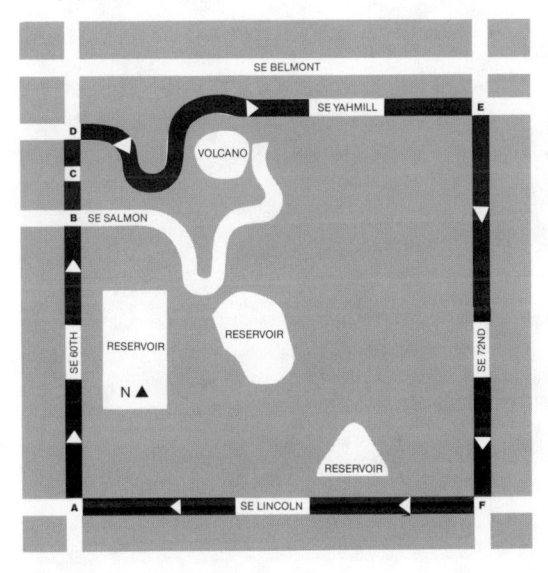

PORTLAND STEP-BY-STEP

63

This is a residential neighborhood and will offer some good views of the city.

D. Turn east on Southeast Yamhill to Southeast Seventy Second Avenue.

The walk from Sixtieth Avenue to Seventy Second Avenue winds around the north slope of Mt. Tabor.

E. Turn south on Southeast Seventy Second to Southeast Lincoln Street.

How did Mt. Tabor get its name?

A pioneer settler, Plympton Kelly, whose father lived on the south slope, named the park. Kelly, an Indian fighter and ardent student of history, was impressed by an account of a battle in the book *Napoleon and His Marshals* by J.T. Headley, in which the French fought the Moslems near the base of Mt. Tabor in Palestine. He decided to give the butte near his father's home the same name. The hill on which Plympton Kelly lived became known as Kelly's Butte.

F. Turn west on Southeast Lincoln to Southeast Sixtieth Avenue.

Return to point of origin.

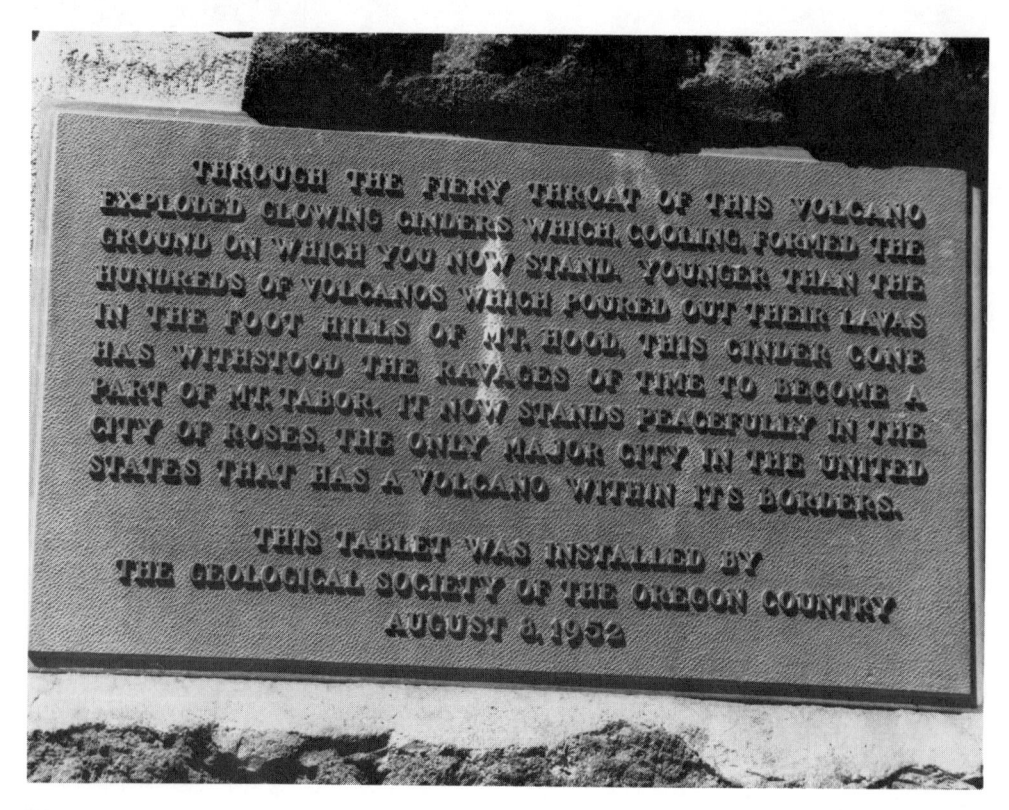

Laurelhurst Park

17 LAURELHURST PARK

Distance: 1.0 mile (1.6K) around perimeter of park plus additional walking trails inside park
Class A walk

A. Begin walk at Southeast 39th Avenue and Ankeny Street.

Here is another opportunity to see a neighborhood in Portland which was designed for gracious living back in the 1900s.

Newcomers to Portland driving east on East Burnside Street are often surprised to see the stone archways at Southeast 33rd Avenue with the name "Laurelhurst" carved into the stone pillar. You expect this pretension to be more consistent with the Portland Heights section of the city, not here a block from a convenience store and other commercial establishments.

This neighborhood is experiencing a renaissance and at one time many years ago was the home of some of Portland's more affluent families. To augment their living style, city officials created Laurelhurst Park, formerly part of the William Ladd estate. Ladd was one of Portland's early settlers.

I admire some of the early 1900s architecture of many Laurelhurst houses. These were homes which, according to records in the Oregon Historical Society, generally were occupied by "cultivated people."

In Terence O'Donnell's and Thomas Vaughan's book, *Portland, an Informal History and Guide*, reference is made to the snobbishness of the early real estate promoters:

"Laurelhurst," said the promoters, "will be entirely occupied by the homes of cultivated people... and everything of any objectional nature will be rigidly excluded."

It was like this for years until the post World War II years when the war brought home servicemen from the war, eager to work and determined to get an education which was provided them by the then-G.I. Bill. They wanted to settle for the American dream: home, family and job. They began rattling the "citadels of the old aristocracy" in such places as Laurelhurst and moved into the fine old homes, turning their backs on suburbia and ranch style living.

To the older families in many established neighborhoods this was an intrusion they would have preferred to do without. However, there wasn't much they could do to stop the tide and soon there were no barriers.

While some of the streets in this district began to slip during the youthful takeover, certain things remained the same. Laurelhurst Park, even the nearby clubhouse where proper music and lectures were held in the early years, survived the change.

To this day the park, which was designed by the same leading New York firm which put together Central Park, has a quiet dignity, particularly during the autumn midafternoons. There are gardens, wooded glens, a shallow ravine and even a small lake.

I walked around the lake on a trail which weaved in and out of hanging rhododendrons. From a vista point east, the lake seems quite small and relatively still. However, when I got closer I saw the lake was a habitat for mallards, geese, also swans and a family or two of turtles, who seemed to enjoy the sun as they rested on a partially submerged log near the center of the lake.

I can see now why Laurelhurst grew around this park and why it set the pattern for the homes of the "cultivated people."

B. Proceed west on Southeast Ankeny.

The walk here is contrasted with the park to the south and the homes to the north. The former clubhouse is midway on Southeast Ankeny.

C. Turn south on Southeast Thirty Third Avenue at Ankeny.

This is about 0.3 of a mile into the perimeter walk. The house at the corner, which some say resembles a sultan's home, is one of the district's more popular and more talked-about residences. It has been the home for years of the Lebanese honorary consul and scene of many gala receptions.

D. Proceed to Southeast Pine Street, then veer left on Southeast Oak Street.

Again, some of the vintage homes which are representative of the district are located here. Stay on the sidewalk which, during part

Lake in Laurelhurst Park

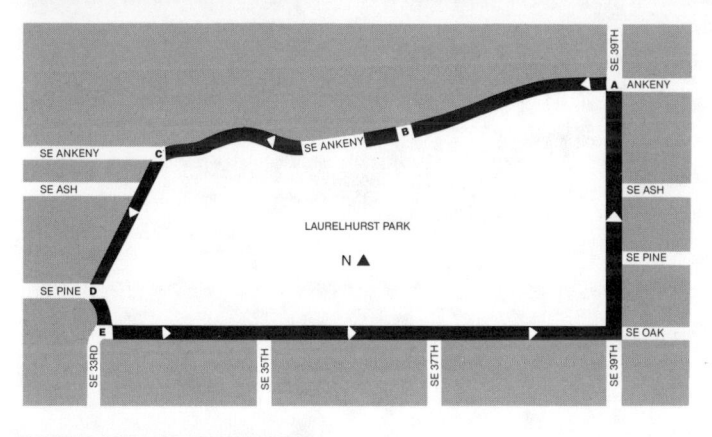

PORTLAND STEP-BY-STEP

of the walk, is on only one side of the street.

E. Straight ahead on Southeast Oak to Southeast Thirty Ninth Avenue, then north to Ankeny.

The walk around the park will serve as a warmup and now the park interior can be fully explored and enjoyed.

Laurelhurst Park

Downtown Portland from Terwilliger Boulevard

18 TERWILLIGER HILL

Distance: 4.8 miles (7.7K)
Class C walk

A. Begin at Southwest Sixth Avenue and Sheridan Street at the northwest corner of Duniway Park.

Despite the comparatively steep climb in the opening leg, this walk has benefits of scenery which far exceed many of the others.

I like this walk not only for the panoramic views of the city, looking east and north, but because it has special memories for me. There also are many interesting stories about the early joggers who earned their stripes by conquering Terwilliger Hill when the word "aerobics" was new to the language.

Reaching the top of Terwilliger Hill, which is about 2.4 miles from the starting point, was a major achievement for the joggers of the 60s. It was the "Everest" of joggers. Nowadays they glide easily over the top and continue on effortlessly to Southwest Capitol Highway and points beyond.

Back in those early 60s, before the "green giant" Metro Y Center was built near Duniway Park, there was an "Early Birds" exercise class at the then all-male YMCA, at Southwest Sixth Avenue and Taylor Street, which has since been replaced by a high rise office complex.

The "Early Birds" met for an aerobic workout on Mondays, Wednesdays and Fridays. On Wednesday, however, the routine was augmented with a 7-mile run which began with a charge out of the YMCA, south toward Duniway Park. When they got there, they lapped the Duniway Park track and then jogged up Terwilliger Hill and back to the YMCA—a grueling 7-mile run.

As a yearly celebration, around Christmas, they did the course on a Sunday as well, topping it off with a hearty champagne brunch at the Benson Hotel's London Grille, one of the first in the city to serve brunch. The event became known to joggers as the "Yule Gruel."

Now, I have to let you in on a secret. There were two joggers who "cheated." For almost a year, two of them—one short and swarthy and the other a little taller and lean—hailed a taxi at the Y entrance and met the others (who were unaware of how the two got there) at the base of Terwilliger Hill at Duniway Park. This was a mile from the starting point at the old "Y." They later repented, however, and promised to cover the entire course always on foot.

In addition to some memories, I enjoy this walk because one stretch resembles the redwoods. The evergreens here are firs and cedars and they're tall, allowing only a thin strip of sky to break through.

B. Continue ahead on the east side of Terwilliger from Southwest Sixth Avenue and Sheridan.

This is the easy part. The path along the park is level. During the late spring this portion is brightened by rows of blooming rhododendrons which border the path. There is a gentle increase in elevation at the first traffic light, about 0.2 of a mile from the starting point.

C. Follow the path to the left, southbound.

About 50 yards from the traffic light, look to the right. Directly across from the service station to the north is a culinary landmark, the Carnival restaurant. Many of the "baby boomers" growing up in the 50s and 60s were taken there for a treat. McDonald's was not yet a household word then. I remember my children wanted to be taken there, not so much to eat hamburgers but to have sweet desserts and sit in the miniature carousel seats. Take a good look. This might be the place to reward yourself after the walk.

D. The hill climb begins.

This is the toughest part of the walk. The next 0.2 of a mile is uphill. Stay alert. The path is a favorite for joggers and bicyclists. As it levels off, there will be the first panoramic view of the city.

Over the years, I have been able to watch the change in our skyline. Back in those early 50s most of the vista was Mt. Hood and the ice cream cone-shaped Mt. St. Helens, which later changed in appearance following its 1980 eruption.

Although the Cascade mountain range still commands a strong scenic backdrop, I find the view of the city below far more exciting.

Joggers on Terwilliger Hill

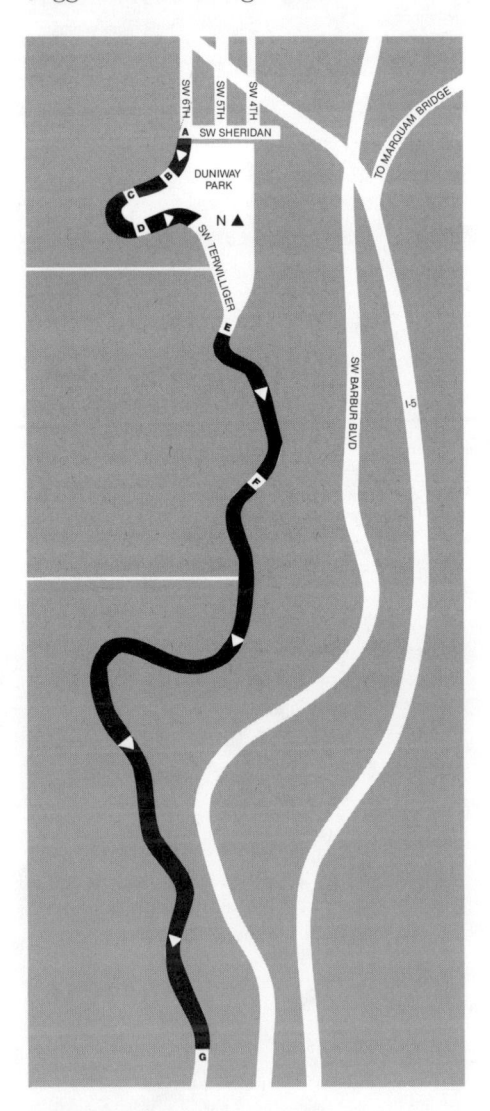

PORTLAND STEP-BY-STEP 71

In 20 years, new bridges have been built across the Willamette River and the downtown skyline has changed from one or two 15-story buildings to an interesting montage of all shapes, sizes and even colors.

E. Continue south on the path.

This is a less strenuous leg of the walk. Allow some time to gather up your thoughts, for the next viewpoint is just around the bend.

As the path turns to the west, there is a gradual incline. This is a piece of cake compared to the hill at the beginning.

This area is the perimeter of the Oregon Health Sciences University campus, which includes the School of Medicine, School of Dentistry, Doernbecher Memorial Hospital for Children and the Oregon Regional Primate Center.

F. Stay on path.

There is another slight incline but hardly anything that will stimulate a bead of perspiration. This is the midway point. The path levels off for about 0.4 of a mile. The distance from the starting point is about 1.2 miles.

This is the portion I referred to earlier, where the route reminds one of the redwoods. Now begins a corridor of tall evergreens which seem to form a head shield from the hot August sun. It's a welcome spot during summer walks up Terwilliger. Take advantage of the exercise course, which is well marked, just to the east, only a few feet from the path. There are hand rings, parallel-type bars and stepping platforms which will speed up the heart beat. A good time to challenge the course is on the return, when less energy is required going downhill.

The last mile to the top is easy and a good time to do some more rubber necking. When the Tri-Met bus shelter is in sight, it signals the end.

Before heading back, walk to the small pond and see the Northwest Indian totem pole. The sculpture, which is more than 20 years old, was executed by one of our leading Indian artists, Chief Lelooska of Ariel, Washington, just north of Vancouver. Lelooska's work is widely acclaimed and during the 1950s and 1960s, he was a sort of folk hero.

G. Turn around, head back.

The walk back to Southwest Sixth Avenue and Sheridan, the end of Terwilliger Boulevard, is mostly downhill: an easy stride should do it.

Willamette River and Portland's near east side from Terwilliger Boulevard

19 MACLEAY PARK

Distance: 3.4 miles (5.4K)
Class B walk

A. Begin at Northwest Twenty Fifth Avenue and Lovejoy. Proceed two blocks west to Northwest Cornell Road, turn right.

There is a mystique about this section of the city which makes it a favorite part of town for many people who move to Portland from larger cities in the east.

One of the features I like, and one which most certainly begins a love affair with Portland, is the proximity of the residential area to vast acreages of undeveloped forest land. Practically at the doorstep of a bustling and progress-driven city is more than 4,700 acres of protected forest. This large stand of timber and woods is called Forest Park—a major part of the largest urban wilderness within an American city.

Macleay Park is linked with Forest Park by hiking trails. These trails are marked and are within a park system with hundreds of species of wildlife.

Don't be surprised if a graceful doe with the agility of a gazelle crosses your path. It is not uncommon to spot these native creatures romping about.

But there is more about this walk which offers a diversity of views. On the Northwest Cornell Road section is a spectacular vista of Mt. St. Helens, in nearby Washington state. It is not designated as a view point but the topography of the neighborhood provides a natural spot for walkers who may want a good look at one of the most recently active volcanoes in North America.

Today, Mt. St. Helens is silent, a stark reminder of nature with all its fury and wonder. On a clear day the volcano with its characteristic flat top is visible from miles away.

B. Continue ahead on Cornell Road.

The street veers to the left, or west, and then intersects with Northwest Westover, which approaches from the south.

There is a slight grade here. The walk passes middle to upper middle-class homes.

C. Veer right on Northwest Cornell Road toward tunnel.

The eastern edge of Macleay Park crosses Cornell. There is a dirt path and a stone wall along the road. Follow this around the first of the two tunnels.

D. At the tunnel, ease to the right and follow the path around the hillside. The path is about 75 yards.

The tunnels were built in 1940 and serve as a link to the West Slope and Cedar Hill communities, which are on the west side of Portland.

E. Cross two small bridges.

The Wildwood Trail intersects Cornell Road at 1.5 miles into the walk. The three buildings to your right are the headquarters of the local Audubon Society. The bookstore is open daily from 10 a.m. to 4 p.m. and on Wednesdays the closing hour is extended to 6 p.m.

There are a number of feeder hiking trails leading from the Audubon property into the park area. This is a popular picnic and hiking area for the urban dwellers of the West Hills.

F. Cross Cornell Road and head back to the point of origin.

There will be the same detour paths around the tunnels for the return trip. Instead of returning via Cornell, however, continue on Westover, staying on the left side of Northwest Westover. The street will take you back to Northwest Twenty Fifth, after a series of several turns in the road. There are equally spectacular views of the city from Westover.

G. At Northwest Westover and Twenty Fifth, turn left.

Heading north on Twenty Fifth, about a block from the turn, are new row houses, the first such dwellings built in Portland's northwest district in many years. At Northwest Lovejoy and Twenty Fifth is the synagogue of Congregation Shaarie Torah.

Trail exit from Macleay Park parking lot

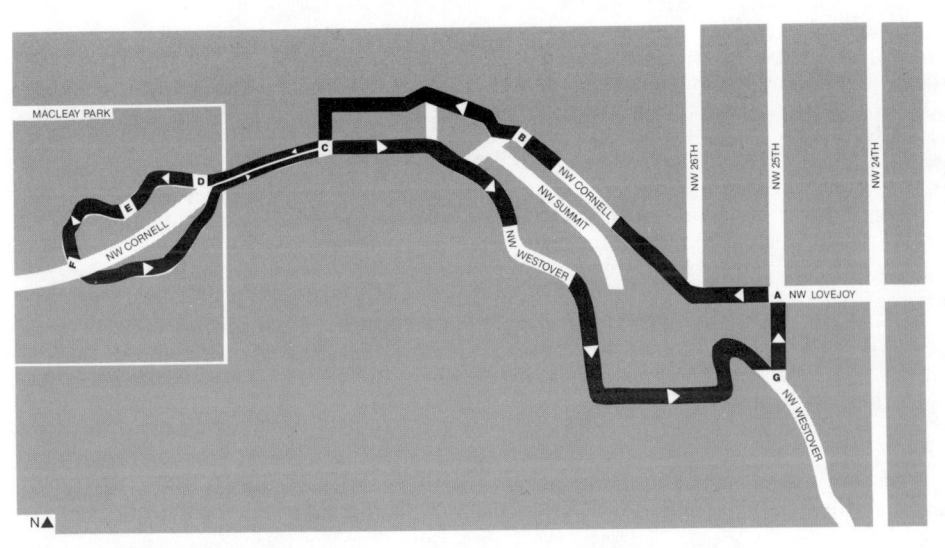

PORTLAND STEP-BY-STEP

20 CRYSTAL SPRINGS RHODODENDRON GARDENS/ REED COLLEGE

Distance: 2.0 miles (3.2K)
Class A walk

A. Begin walk at Southeast Twenty Eighth Avenue, just south of Southeast Woodstock Boulevard at Rhododendron Gardens' parking lot.

Portland is known as the "Rose City." Ever since the famous Portlander, C.E.S. Wood, suggested having an annual rose show back in the 1880s, this city has paid homage to the rose in all its infinite varieties.

However, Portlanders, with all due respect to Mr. Wood, the poet, painter and adventurer, quietly have carried on a love affair with another flower of these parts—the rhododendron. This spectacularly colorful plant which brightens our late spring is found not only in gardens throughout the city but also thrives in a natural state on higher elevations, on the foothills of Mt. Hood. It is so profuse and so revered that a group of citizens living near Mt. Hood chose to name their community after the plant.

And that's not all. While Portland is known for its International Rose Test Gardens in Washington Park, rhododendron lovers have their own sanctuary in the Eastmoreland District. It is unobtrusively located in a neighborhood where the focus is more on a college, its campus, a golf course and quiet upper middle class living. It is the Rhododendron Gardens in Crystal Springs. There are more then 2,000 rhododendron shrubs and their kin, the azaleas, in these gardens.

An interesting sidelight is that for many years, Portlanders, and even visitors to the city, visited not only the Rhododendron Gardens but a nearby commercial establishment, Lambert Gardens.

The Lambert Gardens were owned by Andrew B. Lambert, a transplanted Georgian. They covered some 30 acres bordering on Southeast Twenty Eighth Avenue, bounded at the north by Southeast Schiller, to the south by Southeast Steele and to the east by Southeast Thirty First. The area is now an apartment complex.

It was there for almost 40 years, from 1926 to 1965, and to Portlanders it was a version of Victoria's famous Butchart Gardens. Lambert was a landscape architect. When he came to Portland he realized the opportunity when he saw the site, which at one time was a produce garden, tended and owned by a local, industrious Chinese farmer.

Lambert purchased the property and developed and created a series of 10 gardens, each with a different theme. There was an English garden, a French, an Italian, a Spanish and even a sunken garden. A favorite for the visitors were the peacocks, flamingos and some rare cranes which added a further touch of elegance to the setting. In the late '60s, however, Lambert decided to sell the gardens. It was a period of apartment building—a new generation was in need of housing. Developers bought the gardens and built upscale apartments called the Habitat, named after the apartment living exhibit at the International Exposition in Montreal in 1963.

B. Begin walk from parking lot.

There is a small drinking fountain, similar to the ones seen in downtown Portland. A plaque at the base of the fountain contains a brief description of the gardens by Dean Collins, a noted writer on horticultural subjects who worked for the *Oregon Journal* and *The Oregonian*.

About 50 feet to the left of the fountain is a small bridge which spans a creek feeding the lake.

C. Proceed ahead.

Across the bridge is the main path straight ahead. However, there is a small garden detour to the left which leads to the Jane R. Martin sunken garden. It is a short distance, less than 100 yards, and the garden for the most part is visible from the bridge.

D. Stay right on main path to two sign posts which read: ISLAND, to the left, and PENINSULA, to the right.

Follow the ISLAND path across another bridge which is slightly longer than the first and which goes by a large green garden shed and a small meadow. The path turns and gradually returns to the signpost. Now, take the PENINSULA path. It winds along the small narrow lake and the 17th hole of the

PORTLAND STEP-BY-STEP

Rhododendron Gardens, Crystal Springs Park

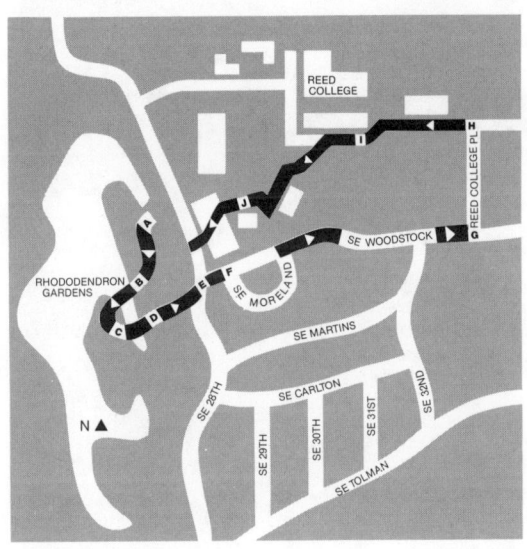

PORTLAND STEP-BY-STEP 77

Eastmoreland golf course is visible. The entire walk through the garden is slightly over a mile.

E. Return to Southeast Twenty Eighth and walk south about 125 steps to a stop sign. Cross Southeast Twenty Eighth at Woodstock to south side of Woodstock to sidewalk.

This is part of the Eastmoreland residential district. Reed College is on the north side of Woodstock.

Walking east on Southeast Woodstock, about 50 feet from the intersection is a small street, Southeast Moreland Lane. This embraces a small colony of upper middle class homes.

F. Take Southeast Moreland Lane. It is about 1/8 of a mile and loops back to Southeast Woodstock.

G. Continue east on Woodstock to Reed College Place.

The main entrance of Reed College is approximately one-half mile from Southeast Twenty Eighth and Woodstock.

Reed College is one of the older private schools in the Northwest and is nationally known for its high number of Rhodes Scholars. For many years during the student upheaval of the '60s and early '70s Reed College was the center in the U.S. for the revival of the art of beautiful writing, known as calligraphy.

The late Professor Lloyd Reynolds became internationally known and through his efforts Portland schools began teaching calligraphy to students.

The names on the old dormitory entrances were done by a friend of Reynolds, calligrapher Father Edward M. Catich of Iowa, who incised the names in "Trajan" capital letters.

H. Take main path to library and stay left. The campus directory is near the entrance of the Vollum College Center.

The Vollum Center was named after the Portland founder of Tektronix, Howard Vollum, who, with his wife, provided the funds for the center.

I. Stay left along the old dorms. Pass by Winch, Quincy, Doyle, Kerr, Abington. Take the smaller path near the Kerr dorm which leads to the southwest between the

Anna Mann and MacNaughton buildings.

This is only a portion of the Reed College campus. The tennis courts are seen to the right of MacNaughton Hall and the Portland west hills can be seen in the background.

J. Pass the Foster Dorms to the lower west parking lot, which is on Southeast Twenty Eighth, directly across from the Rhododendron Gardens parking lot.

The Reed College walk is one mile.

Joe Bianco

Author, editor, award-winning journalist, newspaperman, civic leader, outdoorsman, world traveler, fitness consultant, environmentalist, all these only begin to describe affable, energetic, multi-faceted Joe Bianco.

This is the fourth book from the facile pen of Bianco, who, it seems, reaches into a new area every time he sits at the typewriter. Previous efforts were *Seeing Portland, My Dear Italian Mother's Peasant Recipes,* and *Mt. St. Helens: The Volcano.* The latter has sold 200,000 copies to date.

Among awards are a Peabody for a TV documentary on the 1980 earthquake in Italy, a B'nai B'rith Human Rights Award, and two awards for his work on environmental concerns: The Thomas L. Stokes Award and the Izaak Walton League Award. He holds an honorary Doctorate from the University of Portland.

Emigré from East Coast origins, Bianco came to Portland as a young newspaper reporter for *The Oregonian.* He covered every beat from police to automotive to agriculture until 1965, when his employers tapped him to establish a Sunday Northwest Magazine section. After 17½ years, he was elevated to his present position, where he works on administrative news concerns.

Along the way, Bianco has been elected National President of the American Newspaper Association of Sunday and Feature Editors and Vice President of the American Agricultural Newspapers Editors Association.

Besides being an enthusiastic walker, jogger, skier, hiker and bicyclist, he has found time to serve on the Boards of many civic and cultural organizations. While a Board Director of the YMCA, he introduced and taught agua-calisthenics. He was a founding director of the Oregon Karate Association, is a member of Mazamas outdoor club, Cascade Ski Club and the American Volkswalking Association, U.S. branch of a world-wide walking organization.

Bianco lives and writes in historic Northwest Portland, serene amid an environment of antique and Italian modern furniture, stimulated by an art collection which leans heavily toward local painters.

acknowledgments:

I would like to express my gratitude to those who understood why I wrote this book and to those who liked the idea. It might have stayed just an idea had it not been for the encouragement, both warm and practical, of my publisher and editor, Oral Bullard.

My special thanks go to a fellow writer, Art Chenoweth, who painstakingly inputted my long hand into his P.C., and double checked my material.

I will not forget the help I received from the staffs and publications of the Portland Visitors Bureau, the Portland Chamber of Commerce, Portland Parks and Recreation, the Multnomah County Library, The Oregon Historical Society and its outstanding director Thomas Vaughan and most able historian and writer Terence O'Donnell, author of an enjoyable reference, *Portland, An Informal History and Guide,* and also the many others who helped me along the way.

My thanks also to *The Oregonian* which gave me the opportunity to better enjoy my city and my state.

And last but definitely not the least, to my son, Joseph "Joey" Gault Bianco, who unselfishly gave of his time to photograph the walks.

cover photos: (clockwise from the top)
Willamette River, Hawthorne Bridge and Portland Skyline
Skidmore Fountain and Ankeny Square
The Grotto
Portlandia